So Great
An Honor

Ivory J Harris

10-21-00

The day I pledged.

SO GREAT AN HONOR

Becoming a Bahá'í

Prepared by the
National Spiritual Assembly of the Bahá'ís
of the United States

BAHÁ'Í PUBLISHING TRUST
Wilmette, Illinois 60091

Bahá'í Publishing Trust, Wilmette, IL 60091

ISBN 0-87743-248-1

Photo Credits: Cover (a view of the Shrine of Bahá'u'lláh, near the Mansion
at Bahjí, Israel), pp. 56–57 (Bahá'í Houses of Worship of Kampala,
Langenhain, Apia, Panama City, Bahapur), Bahá'í Publishing Trust; pp. 9, 12,
15, 19, 21, 31, 32, 34, 45, 46, 48, 53, 55, 56 (Bahá'í House of Worship of
Mona Vale), 58, 59, 60, 62, 63, 65, 67, courtesy Bahá'í Periodicals; p. 11,
reprinted from Nabíl, *The Dawn-Breakers: Nabíl's Narrative of the Early Days of the
Bahá'í Revelation*, p. 58 (© 1932 by the National Spiritual Assembly of the
Bahá'ís of the United States); p. 24, courtesy National Bahá'í Archives; p. 27,
courtesy Javidukht Khadem.

DESIGN BY Suni Hannan

Glorified art Thou, O Lord my God! I give Thee thanks inasmuch as Thou hast called me into being in Thy days, and infused into me Thy love and Thy knowledge. . . .

These are the earliest days of my life, O my God, which Thou hast linked with Thine own days. Now that Thou hast conferred upon me so great an honor, withhold not from me the things Thou hast ordained for Thy chosen ones.

—Bahá'u'lláh

Contents

Preface

The National Spiritual Assembly of the Bahá'ís of the United States welcomes you with great pleasure to the worldwide family of Bahá'ís. As you begin the joyous spiritual journey of living a Bahá'í life, you will undoubtedly have questions. *So Great an Honor* is meant to help answer some of those questions. It will familiarize you with many of the essential truths of the Bahá'í Faith and with the origins, aims, purposes, and processes of the Bahá'í Administrative Order. It also gives a glimpse of the Faith's history and describes the Covenants of Bahá'u'lláh and 'Abdu'l-Bahá. *So Great an Honor* is also meant to help you continue to enrich your spiritual life and to begin playing your own role in sharing the message of Bahá'u'lláh with others. We encourage you to dedicate yourself completely to the Cause of Bahá'u'lláh and pray that you will find the true happiness that comes from responding to God's call and arising to play your part in the advancement of His Cause.

THE NATIONAL SPIRITUAL ASSEMBLY
OF THE BAHÁ'ÍS OF THE UNITED STATES

The Greatness of This Day

By declaring our belief in Bahá'u'lláh we are playing a vital part in the magnificent drama of the renewal of religion and the spiritual revitalization of humankind. But what does that mean? And why do we need religion?

The Spiritual Revitalization of the Planet

Bahá'u'lláh likens the day in which we live to the spring, a season of birth, growth, and renewal:

> O My servants! It behoveth you to refresh and revive your souls through the gracious favors which, in this Divine, this soul-stirring Springtime, are being showered upon you. The Day Star of His great glory hath shed its radiance upon you, and the clouds of His limitless grace have overshadowed you. How high the reward of him that hath not deprived himself of so great a bounty, nor failed to recognize the beauty of his Best-Beloved in this, His new attire.

The Source of Religion

Just as every living thing on earth requires the light and warmth of the sun for its existence, our souls need the spiritual light and life that come from God. From time to time throughout human history, God has sent divine Messengers, or Manifestations of God, Who bring the spiritual light that nourishes our souls. Like the rays of the sun that give life to the earth, the Manifestations of God bring fresh outpourings of God's light, giving life to human souls. Through Their teachings and by Their example the Manifestations of God awaken and develop the spiritual life of humankind. Each Manifestation of God brings a divine revelation from God that becomes the basis of a new religion.

The Oneness of the Manifestations of God

Among the Manifestations of God Who have come to guide us are Abraham, Krishna, Moses, Zoroaster, Buddha, Christ, Muḥammad, the Báb, and Bahá'u'lláh. The Manifestations of God are not God in human form, but, like flawlessly polished mirrors, they perfectly reflect His qualities. The Bahá'í writings refer to the Manifestations of God as "sanctified Mirrors," the "exponents" of God on earth. They are the pure channels through which God makes Himself known to humankind.

Outwardly, the Manifestations of God appear to differ from one another, but Bahá'u'lláh tells us to think of Them as one, for They

> are all sent down from the heaven of the Will of God, and as they all arise to proclaim His irresistible Faith, they therefore are regarded as one soul and the same person. . . . They all abide in the same tabernacle, soar in the same heaven, are seated upon the same throne, utter the same speech, and proclaim the same Faith. . . . They only differ in the intensity of their revelation and the comparative potency of their light. . . .

Although each Manifestation of God has founded a new religion with its own character, all of the religions are part of the overall process through which God reveals His will for humanity. All are part of the "changeless Faith of God," which Bahá'u'lláh says is "eternal in the past, eternal in the future." Each Manifestation of God brings new social teachings suited for His time, but the essential message of each never changes. The revelations of the Manifestations of God are like successive chapters in the same book, all of them leading toward the latest chapter, the revelation of Bahá'u'lláh.

This Day of God

While every age in which a Manifestation of God has lived is divinely ordained, the Day in which we live is to be distinguished from those that have preceded it.

The Fulfillment of Prophecy

Every previous age has looked forward to, and paved the way for, the coming of Bahá'u'lláh. He is the fulfillment of many ancient prophecies. He fulfills the Native American prophecy that a light will come from the East to unite the whole earth. His voice is the voice of the Great Spirit. To Judaism He is "the incarnation of the *'Everlasting Father,'* the 'Lord of Hosts.'" To Christianity He is "Christ returned 'in the glory of the Father.'" To Shí'ah Islam He is the return of the Imám Husayn. To Sunní Islam He is the "descent of the 'Spirit of God' (Jesus Christ)." To Zoroastrians He is the promised Sháh-Bahrám. To Hindus He is the reincarnation of Krishna; to Buddhists, the fifth Buddha. Bahá'u'lláh indicates that "The time foreordained unto the peoples and kindreds of the earth is now come. The promises of God as recorded in the Holy Scriptures have all been fulfilled."

The Station of Bahá'u'lláh

Bahá'u'lláh's station as a Manifestation of God is unparalleled. He is not only the voice of God for our time, He is God's Messenger to an age of human maturity. He is the bearer of a divine revelation that fulfills the promises made in earlier religions. He is the Promised One of All Ages.

Although every Manifestation of God has a Dispensation (the period of time when His laws and commandments prevail), the Dispensation of Bahá'u'lláh is very special. It is the final stage in a series of progressive revelations that began with Adam and ended with the Báb. These revelations have all paved the way and looked forward to the advent of Bahá'u'lláh, the supreme Manifestation of God.

We are living in a Day that Bahá'u'lláh says is exalted "above all other days":

> Great indeed is this Day! The allusions made to it in all the sacred Scriptures as the Day of God attest its greatness. The soul of every prophet of God, of every Divine Messenger, hath thirsted for this wondrous Day. All the divers kindreds of the earth have, likewise, yearned to attain it.

"The Universe is wrapt in an ecstasy of joy and gladness," Bahá'u'lláh says. "Well is it with him that hath lived to see this Day, and hath recognized its station."

The Coming of Age of Humanity

To begin to appreciate Bahá'u'lláh's station it is helpful to understand the effect His revelation is having on the world. Every Manifestation of God brings about a new stage in the development of humanity. Each is like a schoolteacher who has given lessons suited to the age and maturity of the students. Bahá'u'lláh, the supreme Manifestation of God, has brought the teachings needed for the last, highest stage in the evolution of humanity's collective life on earth—the coming of age of the human race. The birth of Bahá'u'lláh's revelation has released tremendous creative energies throughout the world. These creative energies have upset the equilibrium of the entire planet and endowed humanity with the potential to attain maturity. Bahá'u'lláh has ushered in the age in which the whole human race will become unified and will achieve lasting, universal peace.

STATISTICS

Worldwide Bahá'í population:
More than 5,000,000

Countries and dependent territories where the Bahá'í Faith is established:
233

Localities where Bahá'ís live:
More than 120,000

Tribes, races, and ethnic groups represented in the Bahá'í community:
2,112

The Bahá'í World Community

Evidence of humanity's growing maturity can be seen all around the world. People of every nation, ethnic group, culture, profession, and social or economic class are accepting Bahá'u'lláh's message and joining His worldwide family of followers.

The Bahá'í Faith has more than five million believers in more than 233 countries and dependent territories or overseas departments.

Bahá'ís live in more than 120,000 localities around the world, making the Bahá'í Faith the second most widespread religion after Christianity. Two thousand one hundred twelve tribes, races, and ethnic groups are represented in the Bahá'í world community. The Faith is among the fastest growing independent world religions. Yet the Bahá'í community is also one of the most unified organizations in the world. No other organization of similar diversity can claim that its members are as unified in their commitment to a vision as distinctive and world-embracing as the revelation of Bahá'u'lláh. Bahá'ís everywhere are dedicated to making this vision a reality and fulfilling God's desire to behold "the entire human race as one soul and one body."

The Essential Truths of the Bahá'í Faith

Bahá'u'lláh compares His revelation to a vast ocean in which we must "immerse" ourselves so that we "may unravel its secrets, and discover all the pearls of wisdom that lie hid in its depths." It will be helpful, as we strive to immerse ourselves in Bahá'u'lláh's revelation, if we first acquaint ourselves with some of the essential truths of the Bahá'í Faith.

Religion: The Basis of All Civilization

Among the essential truths we need to grasp are the purpose of religion, its basic harmony with science, the nature of God, the nature of humanity, and the nature and role of the Manifestations of God.

The Purpose of Religion

Bahá'ís view religion as more than a series of beliefs or a set of customs. They see it as the greatest of all means for establishing order and peace in the world. Its unchanging purpose, according to Bahá'u'lláh, is "to safeguard the interests and promote the unity of the human race, and to foster the spirit of love and fellowship amongst men." Religion is therefore the basis of all civilization and the most important source of human education and development. It helps us grow spiritually. It refines our characters. It guides us morally. It teaches us to translate our beliefs into actions.

Whenever the light of religion is dimmed, Bahá'u'lláh says, "chaos and confusion" follow, and the "lights of fairness and justice, of tranquillity and peace cease to shine." Religion is, in His words, "a radiant light and an impregnable stronghold for the protection and welfare of the peoples of the world." It is the cure for the ills afflicting humanity. It opens for us doors to unending happiness because it draws us closer to God and increases the bonds of love between human hearts.

The Harmony of Science and Religion

Bahá'u'lláh teaches that science and religion, the two most powerful forces in human life, are to be in complete agreement. To help bring science and religion toward a state of harmony, we should study religious teachings in the light of reason and evidence as well as in the light of faith and inspiration. We should examine everything in creation, every facet of human life and knowledge, in the light of both revelation and reason. God has given us the ability to reason so that we can recognize what is true. Consequently, we should not ignore any aspect of truth that is known to us. Our religious beliefs should conform with reason. If they do not, they are superstition, a product of our imagination. The Bahá'í writings tell us that religious beliefs that conflict with science and reason are "unworthy of acceptance."

The Nature of God

Bahá'u'lláh also teaches that there is only one God, the loving Creator of the universe. Various religions may call Him by different names, but He is the same ancient, eternal, unknowable Essence. From Him all of creation sprang into existence, and its dominion is in His grasp.

We cannot picture God or His station, and we can never adequately describe or comprehend Him. But we can learn about Him through the Manifestations of God. In the Long Obligatory Prayer, Bahá'u'lláh refers to God as "the Desire of the world and the Beloved of the nations." God is the loving Parent of all, the one goal for which everything in nature yearns. His love enriches us, and turning to Him and learning about Him brings us spiritual joy that cannot be found anywhere else. Bahá'u'lláh tells us "Thy Paradise is My love; thy heavenly home, reunion with Me."

The Nature of Humanity

Bahá'u'lláh also helps us to understand who we are as part of God's creation and what is our purpose in life. All created things, in their inmost reality, are expressions of the qualities of God. But Bahá'u'lláh explains that human beings are the noblest and most perfect of all created things, for we are made in God's own image. Our reality is spiritual, rather than material. Bahá'u'lláh says

> the soul is a sign of God, a heavenly gem. . . . It is the first among all created things to declare the excellence of its Creator, the first to recognize His glory, to cleave to His truth, and to bow down in adoration before Him.

We are also told that "God has created all, and all return to God."

Our purpose in life is to know and to worship God and to serve and proclaim His Cause. Our efforts to fulfill that purpose cause us to grow spiritually and ensure the happiness, progress, and

We are all children of God, all members of one human family.

eternal life of our soul. Bahá'u'lláh says "the nature of the soul after death can never be described." But He does explain that "if the soul of a man hath walked in the ways of God, it will, assuredly, return and be gathered to the glory of the Beloved." Such a soul "shall attain a station such as no tongue can depict, or pen describe." We are assured that the soul endures after death and continues to progress until it attains the presence of God.

This spiritual reality is the same for all of humanity. We are all children of God, all members of one human family, all descendants of the same original race—the human race. Bahá'u'lláh has proclaimed the oneness of humankind, announcing that we are all servants of God created "from one same substance." God makes no distinctions between people on account of race or color. Bahá'u'lláh urges us to exercise the utmost love toward one another. He tells us "to be even as one soul, to walk with the same feet, eat with the same mouth and dwell in the same land." If we are faithful to the spirit of this guidance, we must eliminate all forms of prejudice from our thoughts and actions.

The principle of the oneness of humanity also includes the equality of women and men. Bahá'u'lláh declares that men and women are equal in the sight of God. Because we are all created in God's image, women and men have always been and will always be equal in His sight. No true distinction between the sexes exists, for they possess equal capacity and complement one another in God's divine creative plan. The only distinction God recognizes between people is the purity and righteousness of their deeds, for He prefers those who are nearest to Him in spiritual likeness.

The Nature and Role of the Manifestations of God

Because direct knowledge of God is impossible, humanity needs an intermediary—a divine educator who can impart the knowledge that gives life to our souls. God has lovingly provided such educators in the Manifestations of God. They are His holy Messengers in human form.

However, the Manifestations of God are not simply ordinary people chosen by God to serve as His Messengers. The difference between the Manifestations of God and ordinary human beings is like the difference between the sun and the earth. The sun, by nature, produces light. The earth, by nature, cannot and must get its light from the sun. The Manifestations of God are like perfect mirrors reflecting and radiating the spiritual light of God. Human beings must receive spiritual illumination from the Manifestations of God. The Manifestations are different from all other beings. They are endowed with innate, divine knowledge not acquired in schools. This knowledge enables Them to formulate the teachings and laws needed at each stage of human existence. Bahá'u'lláh describes the Manifestations of God as being,

of all men, the most accomplished, the most distinguished and the most excellent. . . . Nay, all else besides these Manifestations, live by the operation of their Will, and move and have their being through the outpourings of their grace. . . . Human tongue can never befittingly sing their praise, and human speech can never unfold their mystery.

The mission of the Manifestations of God is the education and advancement of humanity. Each is entrusted with a message and charged to act in a manner that best meets the needs of the age in which He appears. Each Manifestation of God teaches us eternal spiritual truths that form the basis of a new code of morality during His own Dispensation. Each has revealed laws and ordinances that have given humanity practical rules for living. In this way the divine Educators quicken our spiritual nature, awakening virtues that lie undeveloped within our souls and guiding human progress. Their teachings, Their writings, and the example of Their actions are the Word of God.

The Central Figures of the Bahá'í Faith

We are especially fortunate to live in this day and age, because we stand so close to the three Central Figures of the Bahá'í Faith: the Báb, Bahá'u'lláh, and 'Abdu'l-Bahá. We have priceless, detailed historical records of Their lives and ministries. We also have Their abundant, authoritative written guidance for the time in which we live.

The upper room of the House of the Báb in Shiraz, Iran, where He declared His mission.

The Báb, "The Gate of God"

Siyyid 'Alí-Muḥammad, known to Bahá'ís as "The Báb," is the inaugurator of the Bahá'í Dispensation and the Herald of Bahá'u'lláh. Born in 1819 in the city of Shiraz, Persia (now Iran), He was a descendant of the Prophet Muḥammad. From childhood the Báb was known for His exceptional devoutness, wisdom, and nobility.

On May 23, 1844, during a period when people in many lands expected a new messiah, Siyyid 'Alí-Muḥammad announced to Mullá Ḥusayn, His first disciple, that He was the Báb (meaning "the Gate" of God), the Promised One of Islam. In the Bayán, which is known as the Mother Book of the Báb's Dispensation, He boldly proclaimed the vision of a new society. He abolished many Islamic statutes and replaced them with new laws, stressing a high moral standard and purity of heart and motive. He also raised the station of women and the poor and promoted education and useful sciences. But the central theme in all of the Báb's writings and teachings was that He had come to prepare the way for the advent of "Him Whom God will make manifest." He foretold the appearance of another, greater Manifestation of God, Who would usher in the age of universal peace promised in every world religion.

The Shrine of the Báb in Haifa, Israel.

The first eighteen people to independently recognize and accept the Báb's station became known as "Letters of the Living." The Báb sent them throughout Persia to spread His teachings and prepare people for the coming of "Him Whom God will make manifest."

The Báb's teachings spread through Persia like wildfire. They attracted many followers and had a dramatic influence on many prominent and powerful countrymen. But the rapid growth of His Cause angered many religious and government authorities, who saw Him as a dangerous heretic and a threat to their position. He was repeatedly punished and imprisoned. His followers, known as Bábís, were brutally persecuted. Over twenty thousand of them sacrificed their lives for His Cause.

After a brief six-year ministry, the Báb was executed under dramatic circumstances on July 9, 1850, in the city of Tabríz. On the day of execution, officers abruptly interrupted a conversation He was having with His secretary. He warned the officers that, until He had said all the things He wished to say, no "earthly power" could silence Him. The officers disregarded this warning and continued to carry out their duties. The Báb and a devoted young follower named Mírzá Muhammad-'Alí were taken to the prison square. There they were suspended by ropes in front of a wall before some ten thousand on-lookers. When the command for execution was given, a regiment of 750 soldiers opened fire. But when the smoke from the guns cleared, the Báb was not to be seen. The ropes that had held Him and His companion were completely severed, and Mírzá Muhammad-'Alí stood alone and uninjured.

The Báb was discovered to be in His cell again, unhurt and un-ruffled, completing His interrupted conversation with His secretary. The colonel of the regiment ordered his soldiers to leave the scene and swore that he would never repeat what he had done. Another colonel volunteered for the duty, and a second regiment of soldiers was assembled.

When guards came to take the Báb away from His cell a second time, He told them He had finished His conversation. He said, "Now you may proceed to fulfill your intention." The Báb and Mírzá Muhammad-'Alí were brought to the prison square again for execu-tion in the same manner as before. "O wayward generation!" the Báb said in His last words to the thousands of onlookers,

> Had you believed in Me every one of you would have followed the example of this youth [Mírzá Muhammad-'Alí], who stood in rank above most of you, and would have willingly sacrificed himself in My path. The day will come when you will have recognized Me; that day I shall have ceased to be with you.

The second regiment of soldiers formed a line and opened fire. This time the bodies of the Báb and Mírzá Muhammad-'Alí were riddled with bullets. But, surprisingly, their faces remained almost untouched.

Today a beautiful, majestic shrine stands over the Báb's resting-place in Haifa, Israel. It is a special place of pilgrimage for Bahá'ís.

Bahá'u'lláh Himself pays tribute to the Báb and helps us to appreci-ate His exalted station:

> No understanding can grasp the nature of His Revelation, nor can any knowledge comprehend the full measure of His Faith. . . .

all things stand in need of His Cause. All else save Him are created by His command and move and have their being through His law. He is the Revealer of the divine mysteries, and the Expounder of the hidden and ancient wisdom. . . .

Bahá'ís recognize the Báb as a Manifestation of God in His own right. He is the Herald and Forerunner of "Him Whom God will make manifest"—Bahá'u'lláh.

Bahá'u'lláh, "The Glory of God"

On November 12, 1817, Bahá'u'lláh was born to a noble family in Tehran, the capital of Persia. His given name was Mírzá Husayn-'Alí. He was the eldest son of a wealthy minister of state, and many of His relatives had held important positions in the Persian government or military. His distinguished family could trace its roots to one of the great ancient Persian dynasties.

From childhood Bahá'u'lláh was extremely kind and generous and had a magnetic personality. He received no formal schooling or training. Yet even in His early years He showed extraordinary wisdom and knowledge. When He was only thirteen or fourteen He became known for His learning. He could discuss any subject and solve any problem presented to Him. Even leaders in the Muslim clergy listened with interest as He explained complex religious questions they themselves could not solve.

When Bahá'u'lláh was twenty-two, His father passed away, and the government asked Him to take His father's influential ministerial position. Bahá'u'lláh chose to forego the life of luxury that could have been His and instead devoted Himself to helping the poor. His acts of service were so remarkable that by the 1840s He was widely known as "Father of the Poor."

Bahá'u'lláh was twenty-six years old when the Báb announced His mission in 1844. Within a year Bahá'u'lláh learned of the Báb's Cause. At the age of twenty-seven, in the prime of His life, Bahá'u'lláh fearlessly identified Himself with the Báb's teachings and arose to dedicate His life to promoting them. He quickly distinguished Himself as an outstanding Bábí leader. He spared no effort and made many sacrifices to spread the Báb's message. A Bahá'í historian recalls that

Bahá'u'lláh "flung aside every consideration of fame, of wealth, and position, for the prosecution of the task He had set His heart to achieve. Neither the taunts of His friends nor the threats of His enemies could induce Him to cease championing" the Báb's Cause.

At the time of the Báb's martyrdom in 1850, Bahá'u'lláh was becoming well known as one of the Báb's leading supporters. Two years later in 1852, two misguided Bábís tried to kill the Shah of Persia to avenge the Báb's execution. Bahá'u'lláh was accused of instigating the attempt because of His position of leadership. Influential members of the government and clergy called for His execution. But Bahá'u'lláh's personal reputation, His family's social position, the protests of some Western embassies, and the intervention of the Russian ambassador protected Him from such a fate. Instead, He was arrested and brought, in chains and on foot, to Tehran. There He was imprisoned without trial for four months in 1852, in a foul, vermin-infested dungeon called the Síyáh-Chál, or "Black Pit."

The House of Bahá'u'lláh in Tehran, Iran.

In the dark and gloomy Síyáh-Chál, Bahá'u'lláh was surrounded by hardened criminals. He was confined in stocks and weighted down with a 112-pound chain around His neck. The marks of the chain remained with Him for the rest of His life. But despite the dismal conditions, Bahá'u'lláh described His experience in the Síyáh-Chál as a period of unspeakable joy. For during the four months He was imprisoned He became aware of His prophetic mission to unify the human race and to establish an age of universal peace. He recalls in the following passage some of His experience in the Síyáh-Chál:

> During the days I lay in the prison of Ṭihrán, though the galling weight of the chains and the stench-filled air allowed Me but little sleep, still in those infrequent moments of slumber I felt as if some-

thing flowed from the crown of My head over My breast, even as a mighty torrent that precipitateth itself upon the earth from the summit of a lofty mountain. Every limb of My body would, as a result, be set afire. At such moments My tongue recited what no man could bear to hear.

Immediately after Bahá'u'lláh was released from the Síyáh-Chál, He was banished from Persia. This banishment began a long series of exiles that were meant to put an end to His ministry. Instead, they served to spread His fame far and wide and to fulfill prophecies found in the Old and New Testaments.

Bahá'u'lláh's first place of exile was Baghdad, Iraq, a stronghold of Shí'ah Islam. He arrived there in 1853, accompanied by members of His family and companions. Gradually, a small colony of Bábís gathered around Him. For nearly ten years He served as their spiritual leader without revealing His mission to anyone. The moral and spiritual changes He brought about in the community earned Him increasing respect and influence. Princes, scholars, government and religious leaders, and other prominent people came to meet Bahá'u'lláh. But His growing influence again made the Muslim clergy suspicious and fearful. As a result, they conspired to have Him banished a second time in 1863.

When word spread that Bahá'u'lláh was going to leave Baghdad, waves of people of all ages and classes began coming to His house to see Him one last time. On April 22, 1863, Bahá'u'lláh left His house in Baghdad and entered a garden on the banks of the Tigris River to better accommodate the great number of visitors and to allow His family to prepare for the difficult journey that lay ahead. For twelve days He stayed in the garden, which was later named *Riḍván,* meaning "Paradise." There He received a stream of important visitors who wanted to pay their respects and say farewell. There He declared His mission to His followers. The exact words Bahá'u'lláh said and the circumstances of His Declaration are unknown, but He refers to the occasion as the "Most Great Festival" and the "King of Festivals." His writings reveal the tremendous importance of His announcement:

> The Best-Beloved is come. . . .
> Rejoice with exceeding gladness . . . as ye call to remembrance the Day of supreme felicity, the Day whereon the Tongue of the

Ancient of Days hath spoken, as He departed from His House, proceeding to the Spot from which He shed upon the whole of creation the splendors of His name, the All-Merciful. . . . Were We to reveal the secrets of that Day, all they that dwell on earth and in the heavens would swoon away and die. . . .

During Bahá'u'lláh's last days in Baghdad, rather than being sad or discouraged, He showed the greatest joy, dignity, and power. His followers became happy and enthusiastic. Today Bahá'ís annually celebrate the twelve days Bahá'u'lláh spent in the Riḍván Garden as the most joyous of festivals.

From Baghdad, Bahá'u'lláh was banished to Constantinople (now Istanbul), the capital of the Turkish empire. He was to remain there only a short time. His enemies feared that the respect and loyalty He had won in Baghdad would arise again in Constantinople, where it would pose an even greater threat to their position. They soon conspired to have Him sent farther west to the city of Adrianople (now Edirne, Turkey).

The five years Bahá'u'lláh spent in Adrianople were a period of intense activity. He began publicly proclaiming His worldwide mission through a series of letters addressed to the kings and rulers of the world. His reputation and following continued to grow. In these important letters, He announced the dawn of the long-awaited age of universal peace. He proclaimed Himself to be the Bearer of a new message and power from God that would transform the world. But He also warned that there would be great social and political upheaval. He urged the kings and rulers to make the change easier by ensuring justice. He called for the world's leaders to work together to establish lasting peace. Bahá'u'lláh revealed so many verses so rapidly during this time that He kept a number of secretaries busy day and night recording them, and still they could not keep up with Him. During this period in Adrianople, Bahá'u'lláh's followers began using the greeting *Alláh-u-Abhá* (meaning "God, the All-Glorious") with one another. It is a form of Bahá'u'lláh's name and is referred to as the Greatest Name.

Further plotting by Bahá'u'lláh's enemies brought about a fourth and final banishment. In 1868 He was sent to the walled prison-city of Akka, Palestine. Akka was a penal colony to which murderers, highway robbers, and political agitators were sent from all over the Turkish empire. It had no source of fresh water within its gates and was notorious for being flea-infested, damp, and filthy. It had a reputation for being more desolate, unsightly, and detestable than any other city. According to a popular saying, Akka's air was so putrid that a bird flying over it would drop dead.

Bahá'u'lláh spent the remaining twenty-four years of His life in the city of Akka and the surrounding area. He continued proclaiming His mission and revealing the teachings that set forth the laws and ordinances and the basic tenets and principles of His Dispensation. In Akka in 1873, Bahá'u'lláh wrote the Kitáb-i-Aqdas (the Most Holy Book). It is a work of unique importance among the more than one hundred volumes of sacred writings He revealed. It is the principal repository of His laws and is known as the Mother Book of His Dispensation.

On May 29, 1892, at the age of seventy-five, Bahá'u'lláh, the most precious Being ever to have drawn breath on this planet, ascended. His earthly remains were buried next to the mansion of Bahjí (meaning "Place of Delight"), where He had spent His last years. His shrine at Bahjí is the *Qiblih* (Arabic for "Point of Adoration"). It is the most holy spot on earth and the point to which Bahá'ís turn when praying.

Bahá'u'lláh is known by many titles, including the Blessed Beauty, the Ancient Beauty, the Word, the Wronged One, the Promised One, the Spirit of Truth, and many others referring to His divine station.

'Abdu'l-Bahá, "The Servant of Glory"

The last Tablet Bahá'u'lláh revealed before His passing was His will and testament, which He called the Book of the Covenant. In this extraordinary document Bahá'u'lláh appointed His eldest son, 'Abdu'l-Bahá, as His Successor and the divinely inspired authoritative Interpreter of His writings.

'Abdu'l-Bahá was born on May 23, 1844, the very same night on which the Báb declared His mission to Mullá Ḥusayn. As a child, 'Abdu'l-Bahá recognized His Father's true station as the Promised One the Bábís were awaiting, even before it was openly revealed. He shared in Bahá'u'lláh's banishments and exiles and eventually served as His secretary. As 'Abdu'l-Bahá grew older, He became Bahá'u'lláh's closest companion and protector and carried out a great deal of important work on His behalf.

Like Bahá'u'lláh, 'Abdu'l-Bahá spent many years in prison. He wrote a number of books and penned many letters to Bahá'ís around the world to explain His Father's teachings. When He was freed from prison, He visited Europe and North America to establish the Faith there. Upon Bahá'u'lláh's ascension in 1892, 'Abdu'l-Bahá became the Head of the Bahá'í Faith. He served in that capacity until His own passing in 1921.

Throughout His life 'Abdu'l-Bahá was known outside the Bahá'í community as 'Abbás Effendi ('Abbás was His given name, and Effendi is the Turkish equivalent of "sir" or "mister"). To Bahá'ís He became known as "the Master," a title He earned by virtue of His extraordinary selflessness, knowledge, wisdom, and humility, as well as Bahá'u'lláh's own obvious esteem. Bahá'u'lláh surnamed 'Abdu'l-Bahá the "'Most Great Branch'" and refers to Him in the Kitáb-i-Aqdas as the one "Whom God hath purposed, Who hath branched from this Ancient Root." He chose, after Bahá'u'lláh's ascension, to be known as 'Abdu'l-Bahá, meaning "the Servant of Glory."

'Abdu'l-Bahá, Bahá'u'lláh's appointed Successor and Interpreter of His writings.

'Abdu'l-Bahá's station may be best described by the title "Mystery of God," also given to Him by Bahá'u'lláh. The title signifies 'Abdu'l-Bahá's ability to blend and completely harmonize human and divine characteristics. He is the perfect Exemplar of Bahá'u'lláh's teachings, for He embodies every Bahá'í ideal and virtue. He is like a stainless mirror that reflects the light of Bahá'u'lláh. Although 'Abdu'l-Bahá is not a Manifestation of God, He holds a very special station. His writings and utterances have the same authority as those of Bahá'u'lláh. He is the Center and Pivot of Bahá'u'lláh's Covenant.

The New Covenant

One of the most distinctive characteristics of the Bahá'í Dispensation is the new Covenant that now exists between God and humanity. This Covenant is at the heart of what it means to be a Bahá'í. The more we understand the Covenant, the more we understand our place in God's plan for the world.

The Bahá'í writings speak of two Covenants: the "Greater Covenant" and the "Lesser Covenant." The Greater Covenant involves God's assurance that He will never leave humanity without His loving guidance and our promise to try to live according to His will. Each Manifestation of God renews the Greater Covenant when He promises that another Manifestation of God will appear in the fullness of time and calls for us to accept the next revelation. The "Lesser Covenant" is the agreement a Manifestation of God makes with His followers, requiring them to accept His appointed successor after Him. If they accept the successor, the Faith remains united and pure. If they do not, the Faith becomes divided and loses its power.

The Covenant of Bahá'u'lláh

Bahá'u'lláh renewed the Greater Covenant through His own appearance and by His assurance that more Manifestations of God will appear in the future. However, He tells us that the next Manifestation of God will not appear before at least a "full thousand years" have passed.

Bahá'u'lláh has also made a Lesser Covenant with His followers. The Lesser Covenant ensures the continued flow of divine guidance, the unity of the Faith, and the integrity and flexibility of its teachings. In the Book of the Covenant, Bahá'u'lláh's last will and testament, He clearly and indisputably appoints 'Abdu'l-Bahá as His Successor and the Center of His Covenant. All must obey and turn to 'Abdu'l-Bahá, for He is the Interpreter of Bahá'u'lláh's writings. Through this appointment Bahá'u'lláh has safeguarded the Bahá'í Faith against division, making it impossible for anyone to create a faction or sect. This is the fulfillment of the Biblical prophecy about the Day that shall not be followed by Night.

The Will and Testament of 'Abdu'l-Bahá

'Abdu'l-Bahá has preserved and extended the Covenant of Bahá'u'lláh through His own Will and Testament. In that document He names as His twin successors the Guardian and the Universal House of Justice and appoints Shoghi Effendi, His oldest grandson, as Guardian of the Faith. The Guardian is made the authoritative Interpreter of the Bahá'í teachings. The Universal House of Justice is given the function of legislating on matters not specifically addressed in the writings of Bahá'u'lláh, 'Abdu'l-Bahá, or Shoghi Effendi.

Our Response to the Covenant

When we declare our belief in Bahá'u'lláh, we become a party to His Covenant and accept His revelation in its entirety. Occasionally, a

'Abdu'l-Bahá, the Center of the Covenant.

person who has declared his or her belief in Bahá'u'lláh turns around and attacks Him or the institutions designated as the infallible source of divine guidance after His passing. A person who does so is known as a Covenant-breaker. However, we should avoid using the term casually, because only the Head of the Faith can designate a person to be a Covenant-breaker. Covenant-breaking is not rejecting or ignoring Bahá'u'lláh's station. It is not losing or having doubts about one's belief. It is not merely disobeying Bahá'í law. Covenant-breaking is far more serious because it threatens the foundation of the unity of humankind. It jeopardizes the life of the Bahá'í Faith and the achievement of God's purpose for humanity. A Bahá'í who breaks the Covenant is declared a Covenant-breaker, according to the Universal House of Justice, only after "every effort is made to help that person see the illogicality and error of his actions."

Covenant-breaking not only harms those who violate the Covenant, it can also hurt those who interact with them. To protect ourselves and the Faith from the harmful influence of Covenant-breaking, 'Abdu'l-Bahá instructs us to "shun and avoid" Covenant-breakers "entirely." He also instructs us to protect ourselves and the Faith against such harm by becoming firm in the Covenant. 'Abdu'l-Bahá vividly describes this condition:

> O army of God! . . . ye must conduct yourselves in such a manner that ye may stand out distinguished and brilliant as the sun among other souls. Should any one of you enter a city, he should become a centre of attraction by reason of his sincerity, his faithfulness and love, his honesty and fidelity, his truthfulness and lovingkindness towards all the peoples of the world, so that the people of that city may cry out and say: "This man is unquestionably a Bahá'í, for his manners, his behaviour, his conduct, his morals, his nature, and disposition reflect the attributes of the Bahá'ís." Not until ye attain this station can ye be said to have been faithful to the Covenant and Testament of God. For He hath, through irrefutable Texts, entered into a binding Covenant with us all, requiring us to act in accordance with His sacred instructions and counsels.

We become firm in the Covenant by continually trying to live up to our obligation to recognize God's Manifestation and by obeying His commands. To obey His commands, we observe the spiritual practices set forth in Bahá'u'lláh's writings. Among these practices are prayer and fasting, obeying the law of Ḥuqúqu'lláh, reading and studying the sacred writings of the Faith daily, observing the moral and ethical principles of the Faith, teaching the Faith to others, participating in its administrative activities, and contributing to the various Bahá'í Funds.

Being firm in the Covenant affects us personally and affects our community. Bahá'u'lláh says, "Blessed is he who hath remained faithful to My Covenant, and whom the things of the world have not kept back from attaining My court of holiness." When we are firm in the Covenant, 'Abdu'l-Bahá explains, the confirmations of Bahá'u'lláh surround us on "all sides," and we grow spiritually. Shoghi Effendi refers to firmness in the Covenant as our "Fortress" and "greatest protection." It gives us the spiritual strength to overcome difficulties and unifies and strengthens the Bahá'í community. The Universal House of Justice explains that, ultimately,

> The Covenant is the "axis of the oneness of the world of humanity" because it preserves the unity and integrity of the Faith itself and protects it from being disrupted by individuals who are convinced that only their understanding of the Teachings is the right one—a fate that has overcome all past Revelations.

The Bahá'í Administrative Order

While creating the instrument of the Covenant to preserve the unity of the Bahá'í Faith, Bahá'u'lláh also set forth a plan for worldwide solidarity. Its name is the World Order of Bahá'u'lláh, and it is destined to embrace all of humanity in the fullness of time. Its nucleus and pattern is the present Bahá'í Administrative Order, which governs the affairs of the Bahá'í world community.

The Bahá'í Administrative Order is different from any other religious or governmental system in the history of the world. No thinker, no social scientist, nor even any other Manifestation of God has ever created anything like it. Bahá'u'lláh alludes to the power and majesty it is destined to manifest: "The world's equilibrium hath been upset through the vibrating influence of this most great, this new World Order. Mankind's ordered life hath been revolutionized through the agency of this unique, this wondrous System—the like of which mortal eyes have never seen."

The Bahá'í Administrative Order is founded on God's purpose for humanity today. Its source is Bahá'u'lláh Himself. He has revealed its principles, established its institutions, and ordained its operations and functions in the Kitáb-i-Aqdas (the Most Holy Book), the Tablet of Carmel, and the Book of the Covenant. 'Abdu'l-Bahá, in turn, has unveiled its character, reaffirmed its basis, supplemented its principles, asserted its indispensability, and enumerated its chief institutions in His Will and Testament. The aim of the Administrative Order is to establish the Kingdom of God on earth. It is working to bring about and maintain an entirely new mode of community life built on love, unity, and service to God.

The Twin, Crowning Institutions

The twin, crowning institutions of the Bahá'í Administrative Order are the Guardianship and the Universal House of Justice. 'Abdu'l-Bahá says in His Will and Testament that "Whatsoever they decide is of God." Both are "under the care and protection" of Bahá'u'lláh and "under the shelter and unerring guidance" of the Báb. Thus the Guardianship and the Universal House of Justice are channels of infallible, divine guidance.

Shoghi Effendi, appointed by 'Abdu'l-Bahá as Guardian of the Cause of God and "expounder of the words of God."

The Guardianship

The Will and Testament of 'Abdu'l-Bahá established the institution of the Guardianship. In that same document 'Abdu'l-Bahá appointed His beloved grandson Shoghi Effendi as the Guardian of the Cause of God and "the expounder of the words of God." 'Abdu'l-Bahá refers to him as "the sign of God, the chosen branch, the Guardian of the Cause of God, he unto whom all . . . must turn."

The Guardian's chief functions are to interpret the writings of Bahá'u'lláh, the Báb, and 'Abdu'l-Bahá and to serve as the permanent head of the Universal House of Justice. Shoghi Effendi devoted his ministry to developing the Bahá'í World Center on Mount Carmel, translating and interpreting the sacred writings of the Faith, and carrying out the plans of 'Abdu'l-Bahá.

'Abdu'l-Bahá established the Guardianship as a hereditary office. However, because Shoghi Effendi had no children, no successor could be appointed. When he died in 1957, the Hands of the Cause of God—eminent believers named by Bahá'u'lláh, 'Abdu'l-Bahá, and Shoghi Effendi as the Faith's chief stewards—guided and protected the Faith until the election of the Universal House of Justice in 1963.

The Universal House of Justice

The other twin, crowning institution of the Bahá'í Administrative Order, the Universal House of Justice, is the supreme governing and legislative body of the Bahá'í Faith—the Head to whom all must turn. Ordained by Bahá'u'lláh, its purpose is to ensure the continuity of divine guidance, to safeguard the unity of the Faith, and to maintain the integrity and flexibility of its teachings.

Among the duties and powers of the Universal House of Justice are

- To ensure the unity and progress of the Cause of God,
- To ensure the preservation of the Bahá'í sacred texts and safeguard their inviolability,
- To advance the interests of the Faith of God,
- To enact laws and ordinances not expressly recorded in the sacred texts,
- To promulgate and apply the laws and principles of the Faith.

Bahá'u'lláh promises "God will verily inspire" the members of the Universal House of Justice "with whatsoever He willeth." 'Abdu'l-Bahá explains that whatever the Universal House of Justice decides "has the same effect as the Text itself." He tells us all to "seek guidance and turn unto the Center of the Cause and the House of Justice." Those who turn elsewhere, He warns, are "indeed in grievous error."

In the absence of a living Guardian, the Universal House of Justice is now the Head of the Bahá'í Faith. It was elected for the first time in 1963. Its nine members are elected every five years by the members of the National Spiritual Assemblies around the world at an international convention. The seat of the Universal House of Justice is located at the Bahá'í World Center on Mount Carmel in Haifa, Israel.

The Appointed Arm

Supporting the Guardianship and the Universal House of Justice—the twin, crowning institutions of the Bahá'í Administrative Order—are two arms. One arm is appointed, the other, elected. The appointed arm of the Administrative Order includes eminent, devoted Bahá'ís appointed by Shoghi Effendi or the Universal House of Justice to work individually to protect the Faith and stimulate its growth. It encompasses the Hands of the Cause of God, the Continental Boards of Counselors and the International Teaching Center, and the Auxiliary Board Members. The appointed arm works closely with the institutions of the elected arm in a collaborative relationship to ensure the Faith's progress.

The Hands of the Cause of God

The highest-ranking members of the appointed arm of the Administrative Order are the Hands of the Cause of God. They are prominent, trusted Bahá'ís to whom Bahá'u'lláh, 'Abdu'l-Bahá, and Shoghi Effendi assigned special responsibilities for expanding the Faith and protecting it from harm. 'Abdu'l-Bahá lists their duties: "to diffuse the Divine Fragrances, to edify the souls of men, to promote learning, to improve the character of all men and to be, at all times and under all conditions, sanctified and detached from earthly things." Shoghi Effendi refers to the Hands of the Cause of God as the "Chief Stewards of Bahá'u'lláh's embryonic World Commonwealth."

When Shoghi Effendi died in 1957 without leaving a successor, the Hands of the Cause of God assumed responsibility for preserving the Faith's unity and directing its affairs until they unanimously decided that the time was right for the election of the Universal House of Justice in 1963.

The Continental Boards of Counselors
and the International Teaching Center

In 1964 the Universal House of Justice determined that it could not legislate to make it possible to appoint more Hands of the Cause of God. To extend the work of the Hands into the future after the Guardian's passing, the Universal House of Justice created the institutions of the Continental Boards of Counselors in 1968 and the International Teaching Center in 1973.

The International Teaching Center coordinates and directs the work of the Continental Boards of Counselors. The Counselors' work is to stimulate, counsel, and assist National Spiritual Assemblies and to keep the Hands of the Cause and the Universal House of Justice informed about the condition of the Faith around the world.

The Hands of the Cause of God and members of the Universal House of Justice in front of the Mansion at Bahjí, near the Shrine of Bahá'u'lláh, in 1963.

The Counselors work to broaden the base, foster the strength, and ensure the security of the National Spiritual Assemblies, institutions, and communities within their jurisdiction. Because the Continental Counselors are part of a continental institution, their rank in the Administrative Order is higher than that of the National Spiritual Assemblies. Through their work in propagating and protecting the Faith, the Continental Counselors play a major role in knitting together and strengthening the entire fabric of the Bahá'í community.

The Auxiliary Boards

In 1954, to give the Hands of the Cause of God "adjuncts, or deputies," Shoghi Effendi established the Auxiliary Boards. They, too, are part of the appointed arm of the Administrative Order. When the Continental Boards of Counselors were established in 1968, supervision of the Auxiliary Boards was transferred to them. The purpose of the Auxiliary Boards is to spark and support the Faith's growth and to protect it from harm at the grassroots level.

As the Administrative Order evolves, the number of Auxiliary Board members has been increased and their duties expanded. They work closely with individuals, groups, and Local Spiritual Assemblies, stimulating, counseling, and helping them. Auxiliary Board members also appoint assistants to aid them in their work.

The Elected Arm

The elected arm of the Administrative Order has legislative, executive, and judicial powers over the Bahá'í community. It includes the institutions of the National Spiritual Assembly and the Local Spiritual Assembly.

The National Spiritual Assembly

The institution of the National Spiritual Assembly is established and referred to in the Will and Testament of 'Abdu'l-Bahá as the "secondary House of Justice." This institution bears weighty responsibilities, for it must, in Shoghi Effendi's words, "exercise full authority over all the local Assemblies in its province" and "direct the activities of the friends, guard vigilantly the Cause of God, and control and supervise the affairs of the Movement in general."

A National Spiritual Assembly is formed whenever the Universal House of Justice determines that there is a large enough base of local Bahá'í communities in a country. The nine members of each National Assembly are elected yearly at a convention by delegates from local districts.

Among the duties and activities of the National Spiritual Assembly are

- To stimulate, unify, and coordinate the activities of individual Bahá'ís and Local Spiritual Assemblies within its jurisdiction;
- To help individuals and Local Spiritual Assemblies by all possible means to promote the oneness of humanity;
- To initiate measures and direct the affairs of the Faith within its area of jurisdiction in accord with the directives of the Universal House of Justice by keeping in close and constant touch with the Bahá'í World Center;
- To recognize Local Spiritual Assemblies and maintain membership rolls, and to make the final decision on any case concerning the qualification of an individual or group for contin-

ued voting rights and membership in the Faith;

- To entertain appeals from decisions of Local Assemblies when suitable or necessary;
- To supervise the publication and distribution of Bahá'í literature and the review of all writings pertaining to the Faith;
- To collect and allocate all funds for carrying out its purposes;
- To elect, along with the other National Spiritual Assemblies throughout the world, the members of the Universal House of Justice.

Furthermore, each National Assembly must decide whether a matter lies within its jurisdiction or within that of a Local Spiritual Assembly. It must also decide what matters should be referred to the Universal House of Justice.

The Local Spiritual Assembly

The institution of the Local Spiritual Assembly is the foundation of the Bahá'í Administrative Order. Its purpose, Bahá'u'lláh says, is "to take counsel together and to have regard for the interests of the servants of God" and "to choose that which is meet and seemly." 'Abdu'l-Bahá describes the Local Spiritual Assemblies as "shining lamps and heavenly gardens, from which the fragrances of holiness are diffused over all regions, and the lights of knowledge are shed abroad over all created things."

Bahá'u'lláh ordains in the Kitáb-i-Aqdas that a Local Spiritual Assembly should be established in every locality where at least nine Bahá'ís live. The nine members of a Local Assembly are elected yearly. Among its most important duties are teaching and protecting the Faith; safeguarding and stimulating individual initiative; promoting unity; helping those who are poor, sick, disabled, orphaned, or widowed; and promoting the education of children and youth. 'Abdu'l-Bahá says that "the spirit of life" streams in "every direction" from the Local Spiritual Assemblies. They are "potent sources" of human progress "at all times and under all conditions." We are advised by 'Abdu'l-Bahá not to "take any step" without consulting our Spiritual Assembly and encouraged to obey its decisions "with heart and soul" so that "things may be properly ordered and well arranged" for the good of the Faith.

Shoghi Effendi encourages us to go to our Assemblies "as a child would to its parents" and to accept and carry out its decisions cheerfully, without reservations.

The World Center of the Faith

The heart and nerve center of the Bahá'í Administrative Order is the Bahá'í World Center on Mount Carmel in Haifa, Israel. Mount Carmel has been regarded since ancient times as a holy mountain. Almost three thousand years ago the prophet Isaiah announced, "it shall come to pass in the last days, that the mountain of the Lord's house shall be established in the top of the mountains, and shall be exalted above the hills; and all nations shall flow unto it."

Over one hundred years ago Bahá'u'lláh began fulfilling Isaiah's promise when He visited Mount Carmel. There He revealed the Tablet of Carmel, the charter establishing the world spiritual and administrative centers of the Bahá'í Faith. In that Tablet Bahá'u'lláh called into being the "City of God" on earth. He promised, "'O Carmel. . . . Ere long will God sail His Ark upon thee, and will manifest the people of Bahá who have been mentioned in the Book of Names.'"

In 1909 'Abdu'l-Bahá, following Bahá'u'lláh's wishes, laid the Báb's sacred remains to rest on Mount Carmel. This act established the second holiest Shrine (after the Shrine of Bahá'u'lláh) in the Bahá'í world. Upon His own ascension in 1921, 'Abdu'l-Bahá Himself was also buried within the Shrine of the Báb.

In 1939 Shoghi Effendi transferred the remains of 'Abdu'l-Bahá's mother and brother, Navváb and Mírzá Mihdí, to Mount Carmel near the resting-place of 'Abdu'l-Bahá's sister, Bahíyyih Khánum. This act greatly strengthened the spiritual potencies of that sacred spot. Near the holy precincts of the Shrine of the Báb, these three resting-places were designated as the focal center of the "world-shaking, world-embracing, world-directing" administrative institutions that would eventually form the World Administrative Center of the Faith, the "Ark" Bahá'u'lláh refers to in the Tablet of Carmel.

In 1953, after arranging for the building of a beautiful superstructure over the Shrine of the Báb, Shoghi Effendi set about constructing the Bahá'í World Administrative Center. He made a plan to construct five magnificent buildings in a harmonious style of architecture. They were to be built on a wide arc centering on the resting-places of the Holy Family. The five buildings include the International Bahá'í Archives, the Seat of the Universal House of Justice, the Center for the Study of the Texts, the International Teaching Center, and the International Bahá'í Library.

The first of the five stately buildings to be raised was the International Archives Building. It was completed in 1957, shortly before Shoghi Effendi's passing. In 1983 the second great building, the Seat of the Universal House of Justice, was completed at the apex of the Arc.

In 1987 the Universal House of Justice announced that the way was open for the Bahá'í world to erect the remaining buildings of its Administrative Center, along with a series of terraces above and below the Shrine of the Báb and an extension of the International Archives Building.

The building projects on Mount Carmel are far more than a construction project meant to handle the growing physical needs of the Bahá'í World Center. They have deep spiritual significance. The Universal House of Justice writes that, when the buildings on the Arc on Mount Carmel are completed, they will be "the visible seat of mighty institutions whose purpose is no other than the spiritualization of humanity and the preservation of justice and

The Seat of the Universal House of Justice in Haifa, Israel.

unity throughout the world." The beauty and splendor of the terraces and gardens on Mount Carmel symbolize the nature of the transformation that will occur both in the hearts of the world's peoples and in the physical environment of our planet. Shoghi Effendi says that completing the buildings on the Arc will "mark the culmination of the development" of the Bahá'í Administrative Order. "This vast and irresistible process," he explains, will coincide with the evolution of Bahá'í national and local institutions and with the establishment of the political unification of the world.

The Principle of Consultation

The bedrock of the Bahá'í Administrative Order is a distinctive method of decision-making called consultation. The Bahá'í concept of consultation differs from what most people think of as consultation. It is more than a conference or an exchange of thoughts and opinions. It is a process that enables us to find the truth, to make decisions together, and, ultimately, to build unity. It involves gathering facts and coming to a decision based on spiritual principles and unclouded by personal attachments. Bahá'u'lláh calls consultation a "shining light" that "leadeth the way and guideth."

The bedrock of the Bahá'í Administrative Order is a distinctive method of decision-making called consultation.

When we come together in a spirit of true consultation, we seek to build consensus through a loving exchange of different points of view. "Let us . . . remember," Shoghi Effendi advises, "that at the very root of the Cause lies the principle of the undoubted right of the individual to self-expression, his freedom to declare his conscience and to set forth his views." We must be frank and open in expressing ourselves, but we must also be friendly, courteous, and loving so that nobody will feel hurt or left out. We should gather as much information as we can from as many sources as possible. We are to seek diverse points of view. Even more important, we must not cling to our own ideas. When we express an idea it becomes the property of the group. The group tries to come to a unanimous decision, but if that is not possible, a majority vote can be taken. Once a decision is made, everyone gives it their full support. 'Abdu'l-Bahá explains why:

> If they agree upon a subject, even though it be wrong, it is better than to disagree and be in the right, for this difference will produce the demolition of the divine foundation. Though one of the parties may be in the right and they disagree, that will be the cause of a thousand wrongs, but if they agree and both parties are in the wrong, as it is in unity the truth will be revealed and the wrong made right.

We are encouraged by Bahá'u'lláh to "Take . . . counsel together in all matters," because "consultation is the lamp of guidance which leadeth the way, and is the bestower of understanding." When we participate in true consultation we strengthen our community and promote the well-being, peace, and security of the human family.

Bahá'í Elections

One of the fundamental features of Bahá'í administration is the distinctive nature of its elections. Every believer in good standing who is twenty-one or older has the right and the duty to participate in Bahá'í elections. To do so, we need to understand the methods and principles involved.

A Bahá'í election is held to elect a Local Spiritual Assembly at the same time each spring in every locality where nine or more adult Bahá'ís reside. Bahá'í elections are also held every fall to elect a delegate from each district to participate the following spring in the National Convention at which the National Spiritual Assembly is elected. Every five years the members of the National Spiritual Assemblies gather in Haifa at the Bahá'í World Center to elect the Universal House of Justice.

In a Bahá'í election, the believers come together in a spirit of unity and friendliness. They turn to God in prayer, asking for His guidance and aid. In an atmosphere of detachment and selflessness, they vote by secret ballot for those whom prayer and reflection inspire them to choose. Shoghi Effendi instructs us to elect "faithful, sincere, experienced, capable and competent souls who are worthy of membership."

Such people are "those who can best combine the necessary qualities of unquestioned loyalty, of selfless devotion, of a well-trained mind, of recognized ability and mature experience." Personalities, prejudices, and partialities have no place. Each person votes according to his or her conscience in complete confidentiality. There are no nominations, no speeches, and no electioneering.

Shoghi Effendi assures us that "every Assembly elected in that rarefied atmosphere of selflessness and detachment is in truth appointed of God." When we participate in Bahá'í elections in the proper spirit, we are not only exercising a right and meeting a spiritual obligation, we are preserving the health and aiding the growth of the Bahá'í community.

A delegate to an international Bahá'í convention casting his ballot in an election of the members of the Universal House of Justice.

Non-Participation in Political Activities

There is a stark contrast between the methods and procedures of Bahá'í elections and those of civil political elections. This does not mean we cannot participate in civil elections, but it is important to understand what our relationship to political activity should be.

Shoghi Effendi directs us not to join or to maintain membership in any political party. We may vote if we can do so without aligning ourselves with any party. "To enter the arena of party politics," Shoghi Effendi says, "is surely detrimental to the best interests of the Faith and will harm the Cause." We should use our right to vote while staying apart from partisan politics and should cast our vote according to the merits of those we vote for, not according to their membership in any party.

We are advised by Shoghi Effendi to "Shun politics like the plague" and to refrain entirely from interfering in political affairs. The reason for avoiding political involvement is its divisive effect on society. Shoghi Effendi explains:

> the Bahá'ís must turn all their forces into the channel of building up the Bahá'í Cause and its administration. They can neither change nor help the world in any other way at present. If they become involved in the issues the governments of the world are struggling over, they will be lost. But if they build up the Bahá'í pattern they can offer it as a remedy when all else has failed.

When political controversies arise, we should assign no blame and take no sides. Our main objective should always be to draw people toward the unifying spirit and teachings of Bahá'u'lláh's Cause.

A Prescription for This Age

As we increase our knowledge and understanding of God's purpose for our lives and begin to see the unfoldment of a new world order in the development of the Bahá'í Administrative Order, our desire to live according to God's will grows. Bahá'u'lláh, the Divine Physician for our time, has lovingly given a prescription for spiritual, healthy living. His writings offer clear and plentiful guidance about how God wants us to live.

Becoming a True Bahá'í

For Bahá'ís, religion is a matter of deep personal commitment and spiritual transformation. It is a way of life. Through our efforts to become true followers of Bahá'u'lláh—true Bahá'ís—we ensure our happiness both in this world and in the world to come.

The Role of Religion in Our Daily Lives

The Bahá'í writings explain that when we become a Bahá'í, the seed of the spirit starts to grow in our soul. The seed must be watered and nourished daily by the Holy Spirit. We receive spiritual nourishment through prayer, meditation, studying the Word of God, and serving His Cause. By turning to God and trying to make our lives conform to His will, we develop our inner spiritual life and prepare our soul for life in the next world. If we are faithful to God, our soul will reflect God's light and will return to Him after we pass away.

To become true Bahá'ís and to grow spiritually involves daily effort. Bahá'u'lláh tells us to "strive to translate that which hath been written into reality and action." 'Abdu'l-Bahá explains that a "true Bahá'í" is someone who strives by day and by night to progress and advance along the path of human endeavor, whose most cherished desire is so to live and act as to enrich and illuminate the world, whose source of inspiration is the essence of Divine virtue, whose aim in life is so to conduct himself as to be the cause of infinite progress. Only when he attains unto such perfect gifts can it be said of him that he is a true Bahá'í. For in this holy Dispensation, . . . true Faith is . . . the living of a life that will manifest all the perfections and virtues implied in such belief. . . .

According to Shoghi Effendi, living a Bahá'í life means having our lives "so saturated" with Bahá'u'lláh's teachings and the Bahá'í spirit that everyone who meets us will see "a joy, a power, a love, a purity, a radiance, an efficiency in our character and work" that sets us apart and makes people wonder what our secret is.

Becoming a true Bahá'í is a process of spiritual transformation. It means doing our best every day to live up to the divine standards raised by Bahá'u'lláh. It means trying to make everything about ourselves—including the way we dress, speak, behave, and think—reflect our values and our purpose in life. It means becoming so selflessly devoted to God that at every moment we seek only to do what He wants us to do in the way He wants us to do it. It means translating our love for God and Bahá'u'lláh into action and becoming an eager co-worker in the Cause of God.

The Twin Duties: Recognition and Obedience

To ensure that we grow spiritually and learn to translate our beliefs into actions, Bahá'u'lláh has prescribed the "twin duties" of recognizing the Manifestation of God and obeying His laws. In the Kitáb-i-Aqdas, the Most Holy Book, Bahá'u'lláh writes,

The first duty prescribed by God for His servants is the recognition of Him Who is the Dayspring of His Revelation and the Fountain of His laws. . . . It behoveth every one who reacheth this most sublime station, this summit of transcendent glory, to observe every ordinance of Him Who is the Desire of the world.

Bahá'u'lláh says these twin duties are inseparable, for "Neither is acceptable without the other."

Bahá'u'lláh refers to the laws of God as "the breath of life unto all created things." They are the "lamps" of God's loving providence and the "keys" of His mercy. We can "obey them with joy and gladness," Bahá'u'lláh says, because they are best for us. We learn from the Báb that "There is no paradise . . . more exalted than to obey God's commandments." Bahá'u'lláh also calls the laws of God "the highest means for the maintenance of order in the world and the security of its peoples." Our progress, achievement, and happiness depend on our obedience to them.

As we obey God's laws, we grow spiritually and draw closer to Him. As we grow spiritually, we shed the imperfections that keep us from fulfilling our purpose in life and from enjoying true liberty and true happiness.

Meeting Tests and Difficulties

We may expect, after recognizing and accepting Bahá'u'lláh, that we should have fewer troubles than before. In a sense, this is true. Understanding our life's purpose makes it somewhat easier to face difficulties, and learning about the revelation of Bahá'u'lláh brings us spiritual joy. But our belief in Bahá'u'lláh does not make us immune to the trials and tribulations of human existence.

We are all bound to encounter suffering and hardship. Bahá'u'lláh explains that adversities come to us so that each soul may be "tested by the touchstone of God" and "the true may be known and distinguished from the false." When we look at our difficulties in this light, we see them as gifts and blessings in disguise. They give us opportunities to grow spiritually and draw closer to God. Through tests and difficulties we learn to have greater faith and confidence in God, and we are spiritually stimulated, purified, and ennobled.

'Abdu'l-Bahá explains how suffering helps us grow spiritually:

The mind and spirit of man advance when he is tried by suffering. The more the ground is ploughed the better the seed will grow, the better the harvest will be. Just as the plough furrows the earth deeply, purifying it of weeds and thistles, so suffering and tribulation free man from the petty affairs of this worldly life until he arrives at a state of complete detachment. His attitude in this world will be that of divine happiness.

The best way to approach tests and difficulties is to turn to God and trust in Him, praise Him, obey Him, and continually call Him to mind. We can also protect and preserve ourselves from tests through prayer, which leads to spiritual awakening and mindfulness. Many Bahá'ís find comfort during times of adversity in the following brief prayer from the Báb:

Is there any Remover of Difficulties save God? Say: Praised be God! He is God! All are His servants, and all abide by His bidding!

Responding to God's Call

Bahá'u'lláh lovingly calls us to recognize His station and obey His laws. He prescribes certain basic spiritual activities that help us fulfill these twin duties. Among these activities are prayer and meditation, fasting, obeying the law of Ḥuqúqu'lláh, studying the writings and teachings of the Faith, sharing Bahá'u'lláh's healing message with others, and giving to the Bahá'í Funds.

Prayer and Meditation

Perhaps the two most basic spiritual activities Bahá'u'lláh prescribes are prayer and meditation. It is probably easy to remember to pray when we face tests and difficulties. But for our spiritual health we need to pray and meditate on God's Word every morning and evening. If this is a new discipline for us, it may help to remember that the most acceptable prayer is not necessarily the longest one, but the one offered with the most spirituality and radiance. Bahá'u'lláh informs us that reading a single verse "with joy and radiance" is better for us than reading all the Holy Books of God "with lassitude." He directs us to read the sacred verses in such measure that ye be not overcome by languor and despondency. Lay not upon your souls that which will weary them and weigh them down, but rather what will lighten and uplift them, so that they may soar on the wings of the Divine verses towards the Dawning-place of His Manifest signs; this will draw you nearer to God. . . .

Prayer and meditation are vitally important to our spiritual health because, although God's love always surrounds us, it is up to us to tap into it. Bahá'u'lláh proclaims, "O Son of Being! Love Me, that I may love thee. If thou lovest Me not, My love can in no wise reach thee. Know this, O servant."Although God always knows what is in our hearts, it nourishes us spiritually and brings us closer to Him when we express our love through prayer and meditation. Furthermore, praying and meditating on the holy writings helps us grasp their intended meaning. 'Abdu'l-Bahá calls prayer "the best of conditions," adding that it bestows spiritual life, especially when offered in private and when we are free from daily cares. He assures us that God hears all of our prayers.

To help us make prayer and meditation part of our daily lives, Bahá'u'lláh, the Báb, and 'Abdu'l-Bahá revealed many beautiful prayers and meditations. While we are free to use our own words when we pray, we are urged to use the prayers revealed by the Central Figures of the Faith, as they have a special power and spirit.

Bahá'u'lláh prescribes three obligatory prayers: the Long Obligatory Prayer, the Medium Obligatory Prayer, and the Short Obligatory Prayer. We are free to recite any of them, but each of us must recite one daily, according to whatever instructions accompany it. The few simple directions that accompany these special prayers have a spiritual significance and help us concentrate when we pray and meditate.

Bahá'u'lláh offers the following reassuring guidance about prayer:

Intone . . . the verses of God that have been received by Thee, as intoned by them who have drawn nigh unto Him, that the sweetness of the melody may kindle thine own soul, and attract the hearts of all men. Whoso reciteth, in the privacy of his chamber, the verses revealed by God, the scattering angels of the Almighty shall scatter abroad the fragrance of the words uttered by his mouth, and shall cause the heart of every righteous man to throb.

We may, at first, remain unaware of the effect of our prayers. However, Bahá'u'lláh discloses that, sooner or later, they will affect our soul. Praying and meditating daily puts us in touch with God and helps us receive "the breath of the Holy Spirit," see "the reality of things," and attain eternal life.

Fasting

While prayer and meditation keep us in touch with God on a daily basis, the yearly Nineteen Day Fast is a time for drawing especially close to Him. Bahá'u'lláh bids us in His writings to "pray and fast" beginning at the age of fifteen, a practice that is "ordained by God." We are directed to "Abstain from food and drink from sunrise until sundown" from March 2 through 20. If we are weak from illness or age, if we are menstruating, pregnant, or nursing, if we are traveling, or if we are engaged in heavy labor, we are exempt from fasting. If we are unable to fast, Shoghi Effendi advises us *"'to show respect for the law of God and for the exalted station of the Fast' by eating 'with frugality and in private."*

A letter written on behalf of Shoghi Effendi explains the significance of the fasting period. It is described as

> essentially a period of meditation and prayer, of spiritual recuperation, during which the believer must strive to make the necessary readjustments in his inner life, and to refresh and reinvigorate the spiritual forces latent in his soul.

Fasting does have physical benefits, but its importance and purpose are basically spiritual. It is a symbolic reminder to avoid selfish desires. "Fasting is the cause of awakening," 'Abdu'l-Bahá says, for it makes the heart "tender" and increases our spirituality. As we fast and pray, we focus our thoughts on God. This leads to spiritual awakening and stimulation.

The Law of Ḥuqúqu'lláh

Another way we show our love for God is through obedience to the law of Ḥuqúqu'lláh revealed by Bahá'u'lláh in the Kitáb-i-Aqdas (the

Most Holy Book). Like prayer, meditation, and fasting, the law of Ḥuqúqu'lláh is one of the fundamental ordinances of the Faith. In a message to a believer, Bahá'u'lláh refers to this sacred ordinance, saying, "Beseech ye God that He may enable everyone to discharge the obligation of Ḥuqúq, inasmuch as the progress and promotion of the Cause of God depend on material means."

Ḥuqúqu'lláh is an Arabic word composed of the roots *Ḥuqúq*, meaning "Rights," and *Alláh*, meaning "God." Thus *Ḥuqúqu'lláh* means literally "the Rights of God" and is translated by the Guardian, Shoghi Effendi, as "the Right of God." According to this law, a fixed portion of the value of a believer's wealth, with the exception of certain items, is subject once and only once to payment of Ḥuqúqu'lláh. Similar laws have been revealed in previous Dispensations. Giving alms and tithing were ordained in the Old and New Testaments, as were *khums* (Arabic for "one-fifth of one's wealth") and *zakat* (Arabic for "alms") in Islamic texts. In compliance with these laws, a portion of a believer's wealth, according to financial ability, is offered as a token of gratitude to God.

To be able to fulfill the obligation of Ḥuqúqu'lláh is a bounty granted by God to individual believers. Obedience to this sacred law is a binding and essential spiritual obligation that should be fulfilled spontaneously and willingly in a spirit of joy, fellowship, and radiance. It should be done with perfect humility and lowliness, purely for the sake of God. Demanding or soliciting payment of Ḥuqúqu'lláh is prohibited, according to the Bahá'í writings. Furthermore, the amount that is paid is not important, even if it is a single grain. Bahá'u'lláh refers to Ḥuqúqu'lláh as "the source of blessings, and the mainspring of God's loving-kindness and tender love vouchsafed unto men." "It is the source of grace, abundance, and of all good. It is a bounty which shall remain with every soul in every world of the worlds of God." "The advantages arising therefrom shall fall to the individuals themselves." Bahá'u'lláh also says, "It is clear and evident that the payment of the Right of God is conducive to prosperity, to blessing, and to honor and divine protection." Fulfilling one's obligation to the law of Ḥuqúqu'lláh purifies the donor's property and attracts divine protection and heavenly blessings.

Guidelines relating to the assessment of one's obligation to Ḥuqúqu'lláh and information about the spiritual significance of this great law can be studied in a compilation titled *Ḥuqúqu'lláh: Extracts from the Writings of Bahá'u'lláh, 'Abdu'l-Bahá, Shoghi Effendi and The Universal House of Justice.* For clarification of specific situations and for additional information about the payment of Ḥuqúqu'lláh, Bahá'ís may communicate with the Institution of Ḥuqúqu'lláh, which, in the United States, is represented by the Board of Trustees of Ḥuqúqu'lláh.

Payment of Ḥuqúqu'lláh was made to Bahá'u'lláh during His lifetime and then, after His ascension, to 'Abdu'l-Bahá, the Center of the Covenant. In His Will and Testament, 'Abdu'l-Bahá provided for Ḥuqúqu'lláh to be offered through the Guardian of the Faith. Today, in accordance with the text of the holy writings, proceeds from the payment of Ḥuqúqu'lláh revert to the Universal House of Justice, the Central Authority to which we all must turn. Disbursement of these funds is left solely to the discretion of this supreme institution. Ḥuqúqu'lláh funds are used for the "vital needs of the Cause of God," "to promote the interests of the Cause throughout the Bahá'í world," and for humanitarian, charitable, and benevolent purposes such as "the relief of the poor, the disabled, the needy, and the orphans."

'Abdu'l-Bahá, in His Will and Testament, makes the following reference to the commandment of Ḥuqúqu'lláh:

> O friends of 'Abdu'l-Bahá! The Lord, as a sign of His infinite bounties, hath graciously favored His servants by providing for a fixed money offering (Ḥuqúq), to be dutifully presented unto Him, though He, the True One, and His servants have been at all times independent of all created things, and God verily is the All-Possessing, exalted above the need of any gift from His creatures. This fixed money offering, however, causeth the people to become firm and steadfast and draweth Divine increase upon them.

Deepening Our Knowledge and Understanding of the Faith

Another important activity prescribed by Bahá'u'lláh is that of deeply studying His teachings. He says, "Immerse yourselves in the ocean of My words, that ye may unravel its secrets, and discover all the pearls of wisdom that lie hid in its depths." We are instructed in the Kitáb-i-Aqdas to recite the verses of God "every morn and eventide."

Like praying, reciting the Word of God has a mystical effect on our own heart and the hearts of others. Bahá'u'lláh promises that reciting and studying the Word of God nourishes our souls. It opens the "doors to true knowledge," endows our souls with steadfastness, and fills our hearts with joy. The person who recites and reflects on the verses of God, He says, "truly is of them with whom it shall be well." We are assured by 'Abdu'l-Bahá that no comfort is greater and no happiness is sweeter than spiritual comprehension of the divine teachings. Fortunately, our capacity to understand the teachings does not depend on human learning. It depends only on the purity of our heart and soul and on the freedom of our spirit.

Bahá'u'lláh tells us to immerse ourselves in the "ocean" of His words so we "may unravel its secrets, and discover all the pearls of wisdom that lie hid in its depths."

It is important to study all aspects of the Faith deeply. We are encouraged by 'Abdu'l-Bahá to study the principles of Bahá'u'lláh's teachings carefully, one by one, until we understand them with our mind and heart. Shoghi Effendi urges us to "strive to obtain a more adequate understanding of the significance of Bahá'u'lláh's stupendous Revelation." This, he asserts, "must . . . remain the first obligation and the object of the constant endeavor" of every Bahá'í.

Teaching the Faith to Others

As we pray, meditate, and study Bahá'u'lláh's teachings, we will want to share what is in our hearts with others. Because the Bahá'í Faith has no priests or ministers, each of us has the precious duty and privilege of sharing Bahá'u'lláh's life-giving message. This is known as teaching the Faith. It is the most vital and urgent of all our obligations as Bahá'ís.

Each of us has the precious duty and privilege of sharing Bahá'u'lláh's life-giving message with others.

Teaching the Faith is the only true and lasting solution to the terrible burden of suffering that millions of human beings are bearing all around the world. Bahá'u'lláh refers to our "outward conduct" as "but a reflection" of our "inward life" and describes our inward life as "a mirror" of our outward conduct. Knowing this, we begin to understand that the root cause of human suffering is a spiritual ailment. Until spiritual conditions change, there can be no lasting improvement in human affairs.

The best way we can help those who suffer is to share Bahá'u'lláh's healing message with others. We alone have the divine remedy for humanity's ills. When we teach the Faith, we are bringing new life to other souls and building the World Order of Bahá'u'lláh. Nobody else is doing or can do this most important work.

There are many ways to teach the Faith, and everyone teaches in his or her own way, but the teaching process should always include four basic steps:

1. Finding and attracting receptive souls,
2. Delivering Bahá'u'lláh's message,
3. Nurturing the soul to wholehearted acceptance of Bahá'u'lláh, and
4. Confirming the soul in active service to His Cause.

As new Bahá'ís, we may wonder whether we know enough about the Bahá'í Faith to teach it to others. We may wonder whether somebody else can teach it better than we can. But every single one of us—even the newest Bahá'í—is summoned to teach and to make such activity "the dominating passion" of his or her life. We are, in Bahá'u'lláh's words, "the stars of the heaven of understanding" and "the soft-flowing waters" on which "the very life" of all humanity depends.

'Abdu'l-Bahá calls the time in which we live the "Divine season of seed-sowing." Each of us must become a "heavenly cultivator." We must be the "hands" of Bahá'u'lláh's Cause, for He wants each of us to speed forth and "announce . . . the tidings of this Cause." We should not let any feelings or fears of inadequacy stop us from teaching the Faith. 'Abdu'l-Bahá offers the following encouragement:

> Rest assured that the breathings of the Holy Spirit will loosen thy tongue. Speak, therefore; speak out with great courage. . . . When thou art about to begin thine address, turn first to Bahá'u'lláh, and ask for the confirmations of the Holy Spirit, then open thy lips and say whatever is suggested to thy heart; this, however, with the utmost courage, dignity and conviction. It is my hope that . . . those who are seeking after truth will hearken. . . . I am with you heart and soul . . . be sure of this.

As we tell others about the Faith, we must also strive to make our teaching effective. Shoghi Effendi tells us to begin by studying the Divine Word deeply, meditating on its meaning, and praying for guidance and assistance. This does not mean we must wait until we have thoroughly studied the Faith before we try to teach, but that our teaching should be grounded in the Bahá'í writings and prepared for thoughtfully and prayerfully. Then we must arise and act, relying fully on Bahá'u'lláh's guidance and confirmation. Finally, we must persevere in our action.

Teaching the Faith is a wonderful privilege that benefits us as well as those we teach. Sharing God's message stimulates our own soul and attracts divine blessings and assistance. The Bahá'í writings promise again and again that, if we arise with a pure and loving heart to promote God's Word, He will help us. If we fail to share Bahá'u'lláh's message, we deprive ourselves of the divine confirmations and bounties that come from teaching. The more we serve the Cause of God, the more God blesses and assists us.

Pioneering

Bahá'u'lláh longed to carry the glad-tidings of His Revelation to "every spot on the surface of the earth" and to "each one of its cities." His many years of exile prevented Him from doing so. 'Abdu'l-Bahá also longed to travel far and wide to promote Bahá'u'lláh's teachings: "O that I could travel, even though on foot and in the utmost poverty, . . . and, raising the call of 'Yá Bahá'u'l-Abhá' [O Thou, the Glory of Glories!] in cities, villages, mountains, deserts and oceans, promote the divine teachings! This, alas, I cannot do. How intensely I deplore it! Please God, ye may achieve it."

A Bahá'í pioneer teaches the Faith to friends in Suriname.

With the love of Bahá'u'lláh in our hearts, it is now our privilege to carry His healing message to every person on earth. Bahá'u'lláh directs us to "Center" our "energies in the propagation of the Faith of God. Whoso is worthy of so high a calling, let him arise and promote it. Whoso is unable, it is his duty to appoint him who will, in his stead, proclaim this Revelation. . . ." Any Bahá'í who arises and leaves home to journey to another country to teach the Faith is called a "pioneer." If we are unable to serve as a pioneer, we should try to help someone else who can. Bahá'u'lláh calls the service of pioneering "the prince of all goodly deeds." He promises that "A company of Our chosen angels shall go forth" with the steadfast, courageous souls who arise to become pioneers of His Faith.

Shoghi Effendi urges us not to allow anything to discourage us from arising to pioneer: "Neither the threatening world situation, nor any consideration of lack of material resources, of mental equipment, of knowledge, or of experience—desirable as they are—should deter any prospective pioneer teacher from arising. . . ." We are urged by the Universal House of Justice to "consider the urgent needs of the Cause today" and to remember that "Upon our efforts depends in very large measure the fate of humanity."

Giving to the Bahá'í Funds

Another privilege that is ours as enrolled Bahá'ís is to contribute to the Bahá'í Funds, the life-blood of the Cause. Doing so gives us an opportunity to show our love for God and to promote Bahá'u'lláh's Cause. It is an integral part of the Bahá'í way of life.

Bahá'u'lláh's teachings about the future of civilization promise spiritual and material prosperity for all. However, it is up to us to bring about the unfoldment of that prosperous civilization. God, the ultimate source of all wealth, has given humanity everything it needs for the existence and progress of all. Out of His generosity God has also given us the gift of contributing to His Faith, the only effective instrument for bringing about the spiritual and material prosperity of all humankind. Shoghi Effendi explains, in a message written on his behalf, "our contributions to the Faith are the surest way of lifting once and for all time the burden of hunger and misery from mankind, for it is only through the System of Bahá'u'lláh—Divine in origin—that the world can be gotten on its feet and want, fear, hunger, war, etc., [can] be eliminated." Seen in this light, giving to the Funds of the Faith is more than an expression of our appreciation and generosity. It is a sacred privilege and a serious responsibility. It is an essential act of spiritual discipline and devotion to God on which our progress as believers depends.

Shoghi Effendi encourages us to show our faith and courage by being "like the fountain or spring that is continually emptying itself of all that it has and is continually being refilled from an invisible source." He explains, "To be continually giving out for the good of our fellows undeterred by fear of poverty and reliant on the unfailing bounty of the Source of all wealth and all good—this is the secret of right living." It is "the mainspring from which all future blessings will flow."

Every Bahá'í, no matter how poor, is called upon to contribute freely, voluntarily, and generously. Shoghi Effendi indicates that "All, no matter how modest their resources, must participate." He explains, "The more one can give the better it is, especially when such offerings necessitate the sacrifice of other wants and desires. . . . The harder the sacrifice the more meritorious it will be, of course, in the eye of God."

The spirit in which we give to the Fund is very important. When we give in a spirit of sacrifice motivated by our love of the Faith and our desire to see it progress—when we implore God's acceptance of our offerings—we attract the confirmations of God. Giving in such a spirit deepens our connection with His Cause, enhances our dignity and self-respect, strengthens the effectiveness and spiritual influence of Bahá'í institutions, and ensures our own spiritual progress.

There are four permanent Bahá'í Funds to which we can contribute. All of them are important and require our continuous support. They are used to promote and sustain all of the Faith's work. The International Bahá'í Fund supports the work of the Universal House of Justice at the Bahá'í World Center and elsewhere. The Continental Bahá'í Fund supports the work of the Continental Boards of Counselors. The National Bahá'í Fund—which Shoghi Effendi calls the "bedrock" on which all other Bahá'í institutions rest—supports the work of the National Spiritual Assembly. The Local Bahá'í Fund supports the work of the Local Spiritual Assembly.

From time to time other Bahá'í Funds are established for specific projects. One such Fund is the Arc Projects Fund. It is being used to build the majestic edifices of the Bahá'í World Center on Mount Carmel. Bahá'ís from all over the world contribute to it.

Other Laws, Ordinances, and Principles

As we endeavor to respond to God's call by fulfilling the twin duties of recognizing Bahá'u'lláh's station and obeying His laws, we will naturally be curious about the other laws, ordinances, and principles Bahá'u'lláh has revealed for our benefit. Among them are the following:

- Gossip, backbiting, conflict, and contention are forbidden.
- Everyone must engage in work, through trade or profession, for Bahá'u'lláh has made work obligatory and exalted it to the rank of worship.

- Everyone must obey the government and its laws and must behave toward it with loyalty, honesty, and truthfulness.
- All children must be taught to read and write and be given a spiritual education.
- Those who are able must journey, or make a "pilgrimage," to certain specified Bahá'í holy places if they can afford it, if they are able to do so, and if no obstacle stands in the way.
- Every Bahá'í must write a will.
- The dead must be buried no further than one hour's journey from the place of death and must not be cremated. Also, a specific prayer must be said before burial.
- The practice of polygamy, adultery, or homosexuality is prohibited.
- Using alcoholic drinks, intoxicants, and habit-forming drugs such as heroin, hashish, marijuana, LSD, peyote, and similar substances is prohibited, unless they are prescribed by a physician.
- Gambling is forbidden.
- Carrying arms is forbidden, except under certain circumstances explained in the Bahá'í writings.
- Everyone is advised to refer to the sacred writings when differences arise.
- Everyone is urged to consult competent doctors when ill.

Of course, many other laws, ordinances, and principles are set forth in Bahá'u'lláh's writings. While familiarizing ourselves with them, we should keep in mind that they are intended to bring tranquillity to human society, to raise the standard of human behavior, to increase the range of human understanding, and to spiritualize the life of every person on earth. Sometimes our own limited vision makes it difficult to grasp the wisdom of the laws and ordinances Bahá'u'lláh has given to us. Yet we accept and obey them because we believe His wisdom, mercy, and justice are perfect. His laws are "the Water of Life to the followers of every faith" and "the Lamp of wisdom and loving providence" to all. They are designed to carry humanity forward into a global civilization whose glory and splendor we can only barely imagine.

Participating in Bahá'í Community Life

One of the most rewarding aspects of becoming a Bahá'í is joining the worldwide community of fellow-believers, a spiritual family of over five million brothers and sisters. There are many distinctive facets to Bahá'í community life and countless ways to support and participate in the community's healthy growth.

The Bahá'í Calendar

The Bahá'í calendar sets the rhythm of Bahá'í community life. When the Báb declared His Mission in 1844, He began the Bahá'í Era. One of the ways He indicated the importance of the Dispensation He came to herald was to start a new calendar. It is called the *Badí'* (meaning "wonderful") calendar. It is based on a solar year of nineteen months with nineteen days each (361 days). The Badí' calendar also includes four "Intercalary Days" (five during leap years) between the eighteenth and nineteenth months to adjust the calendar to the solar year. During these festive days Bahá'ís offer gifts and hospitality to friends and perform charitable deeds and services.

The first day of the Bahá'í year is the spring equinox (usually March 21). The months of the year are named after attributes of God.

Month	Arabic Name	Translation	First Day
1st	Bahá	Splendor	March 21
2d	Jalál	Glory	April 9
3d	Jamál	Beauty	April 28
4th	'Aẓamat	Grandeur	May 17
5th	Núr	Light	June 5
6th	Raḥmat	Mercy	June 24
7th	Kalimát	Words	July 13
8th	Kamál	Perfection	August 1
9th	Asmá'	Names	August 20
10th	'Izzat	Might	September 8
11th	Mashíyyat	Will	September 27
12th	'Ilm	Knowledge	October 16
13th	Qudrat	Power	November 4

Month	Arabic Name	Translation	First Day
14th	Qawl	Speech	November 23
15th	Masá'il	Questions	December 12
16th	Sharaf	Honor	December 31
17th	Sulṭán	Sovereignty	January 19
18th	Mulk	Dominion	February 7
Intercalary Days		February 26–March 1, inclusive	
19th	'Alá'	Loftiness	March 2

The Nineteen Day Feast

Once every nineteen days, on the first day of each Bahá'í month, the enrolled believers come together in their local communities to observe the Nineteen Day Feast. It is one of the most joyous and important facets of Bahá'í community life.

Bahá'í community life can be one of the most rewarding aspects of becoming a Bahá'í.

The institution of the Nineteen Day Feast is the foundation of the new World Order. Its purpose Bahá'u'lláh says, is "to bind hearts together . . . through both earthly and heavenly means." Started by the Báb and confirmed by Bahá'u'lláh, the Feast represents a new stage of development in the basic expression of community life. It enables us to contribute to the power of Bahá'u'lláh's Cause in many different ways.

The Nineteen Day Feast has three separate but related parts. The first part is devotional and includes prayers and readings from the sacred writings. The second part is a period of consultation. During this part the Local Spiritual Assembly reports to the community on its affairs, shares news and messages from the Bahá'í World Center and the National Spiritual Assembly, and receives the thoughts and recommendations of the believers. This period of consultation gives each of us an excellent opportunity to exercise our right of self-expression. We should contribute freely and share our views during discussions. The third part of the Feast is a time of loving fellowship that includes refreshments and other social activities.

Although we are not obligated to go to Feasts, 'Abdu'l-Bahá tells us to give "great weight" to them. "This Feast is a bringer of joy," He says. "It is the groundwork of agreement and unity. It is the key to affection and fellowship. It diffuseth the oneness of mankind." Shoghi Effendi refers to attendance at the Feast as a "very important" duty and privilege and encourages us to think of it as "the very heart" of our spiritual activities.

We can help make Feast the spiritually refreshing experience it is meant to be by preparing ourselves for it spiritually. Before entering the Feast, we must free our hearts and minds from all else save God. 'Abdu'l-Bahá suggests that we consider others who are present at the Feast as better and greater than ourselves and think about how we can make them happy. We should strive to be so united that the Feast will become the cause of spiritual solidarity. "If the Feast is befittingly held, in the manner described," 'Abdu'l-Bahá says, it will be "the Lord's Supper" and will attract God's confirmation "like a magnet."

Bahá'í Holy Days and Holidays

Another important facet of Bahá'í community life is the celebration and observance of Bahá'í holy days. These are the days on which we show special honor and reverence for Bahá'u'lláh, the Báb, and 'Abdu'l-Bahá. They include the following:

Holy Day	Date
*Feast of Naw-Rúz (Bahá'í New Year)	March 21
Feast of Ridván	April 21–May 2
*The First Day	April 21
*The Ninth Day	April 29
*The Twelfth Day	May 2
*Anniversary of the Declaration of the Báb	May 23

Holy Day	Date
*Anniversary of the Ascension of Bahá'u'lláh	May 29
*Anniversary of the Martyrdom of the Báb	July 9
*Anniversary of the Birth of the Báb	October 20
*Anniversary of the Birth of Bahá'u'lláh	November 12
Day of the Covenant	November 26
Anniversary of the Ascension of 'Abdu'l-Bahá	November 28

* Days on which school and work should be suspended.

On nine of the holy days work is not allowed. On such days we show our reverence for the Faith by observing the occasion and making every effort to be excused from work or school.

Some of the holy days are festive celebrations (Naw-Rúz, Riḍván, and the anniversaries of the Declaration of the Báb, the Birth of Bahá'u'lláh, and the Day of the Covenant). On such occasions we hold joyous celebrations in our communities. Some holy days are solemn, commemorative occasions (the anniversaries of the Ascension of Bahá'u'lláh, the Martyrdom of the Báb, and the Ascension of 'Abdu'l-Bahá). On these occasions we hold quiet observances that include prayers and meditations.

Bahá'í Houses of Worship

The Bahá'í House of Worship of 'Ishqábád (or Ashkhabad), Turkistan, as it stood before it was damaged by an earthquake in 1948 and demolished in 1962.

Bahá'í Houses of Worship are yet another important part of Bahá'í community life. Like most religions, the Bahá'í Faith has Houses of Worship that are dedicated to the praise and remembrance of God. The title for a Bahá'í House of Worship is *Mashriqu'l-Adhkár*, mean-

The Baháʼí House of
Worship of Kampala,
Uganda.

The Baháʼí House of Worship of
Mona Vale (near Sydney),
Australia.

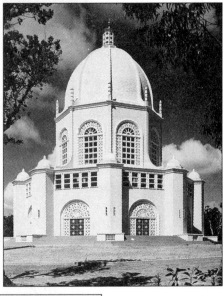

The Baháʼí House of
Worship of
Langenhain (near
Frankfurt am Main),
Germany.

The Bahá'í House of Worship of Apia, Western Samoa.

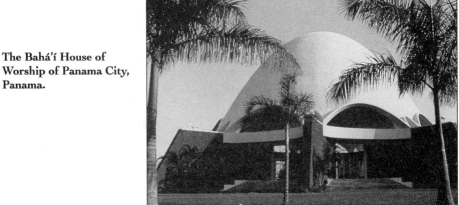

The Bahá'í House of Worship of Panama City, Panama.

The Bahá'í House of Worship of Bahapur (near New Delhi), India.

The Bahá'í House of Worship of Wilmette, Illinois, known to Bahá'ís as the holiest Bahá'í House of Worship and the Mother Temple of the West.

ing in Arabic "Dawning-Place of the Praises of God." Every Bahá'í House of Worship is open to people of all religions. Although each has its own architectural style reflecting its local culture, all share certain characteristics. Each is a beautiful nine-sided circular building topped with a dome. The first Bahá'í House of Worship was built in 'Ishqábád (or Ashkhabad), Turkistan. The building was taken over by the Soviet government in 1938 and was eventually demolished in 1962, after being damaged by an earthquake. Bahá'ís have also built Houses of Worship in Wilmette (near Chicago), Illinois; Kampala, Uganda; Mona Vale (near Sydney), Australia; Langenhain (near Frankfurt am Main), Germany; Panama City, Panama; Apia, Western Samoa; and Bahapur (near New Delhi), India.

The holiest Bahá'í House of Worship in the world is the one in Wilmette, Illinois. Located at the heart of the North American continent, it is known as the Mother Temple of the West. 'Abdu'l-Bahá Himself dedicated its site in 1912 and said its founding marked "'the inception of the Kingdom of God on earth.'" Shoghi Effendi referred to it as "the noblest structure reared in the first Bahá'í century, and the symbol and precursor of a future world civilization."

Bahá'ís eventually will build a House of Worship in every community around the world. Each Bahá'í House of Worship is to form the center of a complex of dependencies that will serve the needs of society. The dependencies will be dedicated to social, humanitarian, educational, and scientific pursuits. This complex of institutions is also known as the *Mashriqu'l-Adhkár*. 'Abdu'l-Bahá refers to it as "one of the most vital institutions in the world."

The Spiritual Education of Children and Youth

One of the most important ways we can support and participate in the healthy growth of our Bahá'í community is to take part in the spiritual education of children and youth. Although parents have primary responsibility for educating their children, the entire community can share in carrying out this responsibility. No matter what our age may be, we can try to provide a positive role model, and we can support Bahá'í classes for children and youth with our time, money, or other resources.

According to 'Abdu'l-Bahá, "The hearts of all children are of the utmost purity. They are mirrors upon which no dust has fallen." Yet, unless their souls are assisted by "the spirit of faith," they cannot progress spiritually. We must train children "with divine exhortations" and instill the love of God in their hearts.

'Abdu'l-Bahá places the education and training of children "Among the greatest of all services that can possibly be rendered by man to Almighty God." It is vital to humanity's progress, for the children and youth of today will eventually be responsible for the progress of the Faith tomorrow. A spiritual education is clearly an essential part of the unfoldment of the World

The spiritual education and training of children is one of the greatest of all services that can possibly be rendered to God.

Order of Bahá'u'lláh. Shoghi Effendi explains that children and youth "who have the benefits of both material and spiritual education will be the true leaders of society." The children and youth of the world have a destiny before God: They are instruments of healing among humankind, and they have a vital role to play in teaching the Faith.

Relationships in the Day of God

Bahá'u'lláh's divinely prescribed laws not only set new standards of behavior and morality for individuals and communities, they also set new standards for our personal relationships with others.

A Chaste and Holy Life

Living a chaste and holy life does not mean we have to be solemn or joyless. Humor, happiness, and joy are characteristics of a true Bahá'í life.

One of the new standards Bahá'u'lláh has prescribed that affects our personal relationships with others is chastity. Shoghi Effendi declares, "A chaste and holy life must be made the controlling principle in the behavior and conduct of all Bahá'ís." This principle guides our personal relationships with other Bahá'ís as well as with the world at large.

The concept of chastity is a challenging one today. But the high standard we are called to is not a form of self-denial or puritanism. Bahá'u'lláh does not wish to deny us the right and privilege of relishing or benefitting from the many joys, beauties, and pleasures God has provided. Bahá'u'lláh assures us that,

> Should a man wish to adorn himself with the ornaments of the earth, to wear its apparels, or partake of the benefits it can bestow, no harm can befall him, if he alloweth nothing whatever to intervene between him and God, for God hath ordained every good thing, whether created in the heavens or in the earth, for such of His servants as truly believe in Him.

Living a chaste and holy life does not mean we have to be solemn or joyless. The Universal House of Justice reminds us that humor, happiness, and joy are "characteristics of a true Bahá'í life." A balanced life includes these characteristics as well as serious thought, compassion, and humble service to God.

A chaste and holy life implies "modesty, purity, temperance, decency, and clean-mindedness," Shoghi Effendi explains. It involves "moderation in all that pertains to dress, language, amusements, and all artistic and literary avocations." It requires "daily vigilance" in controlling our sensual desires and corrupt tendencies. It calls for abandoning "frivolous conduct" and "excessive attachment to trivial and often misdirected pleasures." It requires abstinence from alcohol and other habit-forming drugs and denounces "the prostitution of art and literature," nudism, companionate marriage, and marital infidelity. It condemns all promiscuity, easy familiarity, and extramarital sex.

The importance of upholding the principle of chastity is clear when we compare the laws and standards of the Bahá'í Faith to the physical laws of the universe. When we understand and live in harmony with the physical laws, our lives are easier. Similarly, understanding and living in harmony with the spiritual laws and standards of the Faith frees us from untold spiritual and moral difficulties. Living a chaste and holy life makes us healthier, happier, and nobler.

Marriage

Living a chaste and holy life also preserves the sanctity and stability of marriage, the bedrock of society. A healthy, unified society is built on marriages that are strong and sound.

Bahá'u'lláh highly recommends that we marry "as an assistance" to ourselves. He calls marriage "a fortress for well-being and salvation." 'Abdu'l-Bahá describes Bahá'í marriage as a physical and spiritual union in which husband and wife are "aglow with the same wine" and "enamored of the same matchless Face." Both "live and move through the same spirit" and are "illumined by the same glory."

Spiritually sound, happy marriages require preparation. We need to take time to get to know our intended partner thoroughly before deciding to marry. When we choose a partner, we should do so with the intention of creating an everlasting union. After choosing a partner, we must obtain our parents' permission before we can marry. The reason Bahá'u'lláh has laid down this "great law" requiring parental permission, Shoghi Effendi says, is

> to strengthen the social fabric, to knit closer the ties of the home, to place a certain gratitude and respect in the hearts of the children for those who have given them life and sent their souls out on the eternal journey towards their Creator.

If our parents consent to the union, the marriage can take place.

We are free to plan our own wedding as we wish, in accordance with civil law, but any Bahá'í who wishes to marry must have a Bahá'í marriage ceremony, officiated by either a Local or National Spiritual Assembly. The Bahá'í ceremony involves the simple exchange of a vow in front of two witnesses approved by the officiating Spiritual Assembly. The bride and groom recite to one another the following verse: "We will all, verily, abide by the Will of God." This simple vow reminds us of the sanctity of marriage and of its spiritual basis.

True marriage is a union that improves the spiritual life of both partners and lasts throughout all the worlds of God.

A Bahá'í husband and wife are expected to be absolutely faithful to their marital partner in thought and deed. If their marriage fails and they find it necessary to consider divorcing, they must prayerfully try to rise above their differences. They must try to restore harmony while living separately for at least one year. This time of separation is known as a "year of patience" or "year of waiting" and is supervised by the Local Spiritual Assembly. If reconciliation is still impossible after the year of patience, divorce may be allowed as a last resort. Nonetheless, Bahá'u'lláh strongly discourages divorce because of its disruptive effect on family life.

Because God loves unity and concord and abhors separation and discord, we must try to make our marriages unions "of the body and of the spirit as well." We should try to achieve "true marriage," which, according to 'Abdu'l-Bahá, improves the spiritual life of both partners and lasts "throughout all the worlds of God."

Family Life

The Bahá'í writings tell us that the sacred and primary purpose of marriage is to raise a family. Bahá'u'lláh encourages us to marry so that we "may bring forth one who will make mention of Me amid My servants." More than a joyful and rewarding experience, child-rearing is a sacred responsibility that begins the moment a child is conceived.

In the Bahá'í ideal of the family, each member has a special role to play. Of course, many families today do not match the traditional pattern of mother, father, and children. But the same principles that govern the ideal family structure apply to single-parent families, step-families, and other non-traditional family structures. In every family the parents have the responsibility to educate their children. Children have the responsibility to obey their parents. The father has the primary responsibility to provide for and protect the family, while the mother is the first educator of the children. However, this does not exclude men from training children or women from working. 'Abdu'l-Bahá explains,

All the members of a Bahá'í family have the duty to fill their life together with God's love and with the principles of the Bahá'í Faith.

Just as the son has certain obligations to his father, the father, likewise, has certain obligations to his son. The mother, the sister and other members of the household have their certain prerogatives. All these rights and prerogatives must be conserved, yet the unity of the family must be sustained. The injury of one shall be considered the injury of all; the comfort of each, the comfort of all; the honor of one, the honor of all.

All the members of a Bahá'í family have the duty to fill their life together with God's love and with the principles of the Bahá'í Faith. To help create a spirit of unity, Bahá'í families should try to pray and study the Bahá'í writings together daily. From their earliest years, children should be taught to pray and meditate and to acquire spiritual as well as intellectual knowledge. When a family is united in this way, 'Abdu'l-Bahá says, its affairs are easy to manage:

> Note ye . . . what progress the members of that family make, how they prosper in the world. Their concerns are in order, they enjoy comfort and tranquillity, they are secure, their position is assured, they come to be envied by all. Such a family but addeth to its stature and its lasting honour, as day succeedeth day.

The importance of the family is easy to understand when we grasp its role in society. 'Abdu'l-Bahá suggests that we

> Compare the nations of the world to the members of a family. A family is a nation in miniature. Simply enlarge the circle of the household and you have the nation. Enlarge the circle of the nations and you have all humanity. The conditions surrounding the family surround the nation. The happenings of the family are the happenings in the life of the nation.

If our families are characterized by fighting, disunity, jealousy, and trouble, our nations will have the same problems. If our families are characterized by affection, harmony, and unity, our nations will be, too. It is impossible to unite others unless we ourselves are united.

Race Unity

The same standards that apply to family life apply to our relationships with the rest of our human family. The most important standard to which Bahá'u'lláh calls us is unity. The Universal House of Justice refers to it as "the alpha and omega of all Bahá'í objectives."

Achieving unity in the human family requires eliminating racism, one of the most destructive and persistent evils. Bahá'u'lláh repeatedly emphasizes in His writings that all people are members of one human family, that there is only one human race. The earth is our common home, and racial barriers are groundless and unjustifiable.

Unity is "the alpha and omega of all Bahá'í objectives."

To eliminate racial barriers, we must embrace the principle of the oneness of humanity and make it real in our own lives. We should neither mistrust nor keep our distance from people of a different race or color. Instead, we are advised by 'Abdu'l-Bahá to "rejoice to be among them" and "show them kindness." He encourages us to intermarry among the races, saying, "Thou must endeavor that they [blacks and whites] intermarry," for "marriage between these two races will wholly destroy and eradicate the root of enmity." Overcoming racism and creating harmony, Shoghi Effendi says, requires demonstrating genuine love, extreme patience, true humility, superb tact, sensible initiative, mature wisdom, and deliberate, persistent, and prayerful effort. Whatever our heritage may be, we must abandon any attitudes of superiority, suspicion, or impatience toward other races.

The Equality of the Sexes

Achieving unity in the human family also requires establishing the equality of the sexes. For the first time in history, a Manifestation of God has proclaimed the equality of women and men. All other religions have placed man above woman. But Bahá'u'lláh says, "In this Day the Hand of divine grace hath removed all distinction. The servants of God and His handmaidens are regarded on the same plane." Men and women are equal in the sight of God. 'Abdu'l-Bahá explains that, in the Dispensation of Bahá'u'lláh, "the women go neck and neck with the men. In no movement will they be left behind. Their rights with men are equal in degree." There is no longer any justification for denying women equality.

Achieving equality of the sexes does not mean ignoring their biological differences. Nor does it mean men and women are to have identical functions. Each sex is the "complement and helpmeet of the other," 'Abdu'l-Bahá says. The differences between them are "negligible." What may appear to be inequalities between the sexes are merely the results of denying women the opportunities men enjoy—especially educational opportunities. When women are fully educated and granted their rights, they will prove themselves to be men's equals. 'Abdu'l-Bahá declares, "When men own the equality of women there will be no need for them to struggle for their rights!"

Until the equality of women and men is fully established, 'Abdu'l-Bahá says, "The highest social development of mankind is not possible." He compares humanity to a bird and its two wings: "the one is male, the other female. Unless both wings are strong . . . the bird cannot fly heavenwards." To balance the strength of both wings, Bahá'u'lláh places higher priority on the education of daughters than on that of sons. He explains, "the training and culture of daughters is more necessary" than that of sons because women are the first educators of children. They can, therefore, spread the benefits of learning through society most quickly and effectively.

Women also have a critical role to play in ending war and establishing peace. According to 'Abdu'l-Bahá,

> War and its ravages have blighted the world; the education of woman will be a mighty step toward its abolition and ending, for she will use her whole influence against war. She will refuse to give her sons for sacrifice upon the field of battle. In truth, she will be the greatest factor in establishing universal peace and international arbitration. Assuredly, woman will abolish warfare among mankind.

Although the world has been ruled until now by the masculine qualities of force and aggression, this is beginning to change. False distinctions between the sexes are falling away, and the status of women is improving. The masculine and feminine characteristics of civilization are becoming more evenly balanced. The qualities of love and service, in which women are strong, are gaining influence.

Fellowship

Achieving race unity and the equality of the sexes is challenging. Adjusting our attitudes is an important first step. But to create unity, we have to practice what we believe and change our behavior. One of the best ways to do this is through loving fellowship with others.

The Bahá'í writings urge us to try earnestly to create bonds of fellowship and love with all peoples. Bahá'u'lláh Himself directs us to "Consort with all men . . . in a spirit of friendliness and fellowship" and to deal with one another "with the utmost love and harmony." 'Abdu'l-Bahá has shown us how to do this through His own perfect example. His courage, His sincere love for all, His informal friendliness toward all, His aversion to criticism, His wisdom and tact, His sympathy for the downtrodden, His

The Bahá'í writings urge us to try earnestly to create bonds of fellowship with all peoples.

enduring sense of the oneness of humanity, and His keen sense of justice are the model Bahá'ís try to live up to.

We will surely help to create unity if we try to live by 'Abdu'l-Bahá's advice to "manifest complete love and affection toward all mankind." He advises us not to exalt ourselves above others, but to consider all as our equals and recognize them as servants of one God. He urges us never to speak disparagingly of others, but to "praise without distinction." We should consider our enemies as friends, treat our ill-wishers as well-wishers, and beware not to "offend any heart." We should try instead to "Be the source of consolation to every sad one, assist every weak one, be helpful to every indigent one, care for every sick one, be the cause of glorification to every lowly one, and shelter those who are overshadowed by fear." In brief, 'Abdu'l-Bahá asks each of us to "Be trustworthy, sincere, affectionate and replete with chastity. Be illumined, be spiritual, be divine, be glorious, be quickened of God, be a Bahá'í."

Moving into Action

Through our efforts to become a true Bahá'í by responding to God's call and participating in Bahá'í community life, we will be enabled to benefit, in greater and greater measures, from the divine healing medicine of Bahá'u'lláh's teachings. We will become, in 'Abdu'l-Bahá's words, "as a lamp shining forth with the light of the virtues of the world of humanity." We will be a source of hope for others.

Hope for the Future

The coming of Bahá'u'lláh has ushered the world into a new age. Shoghi Effendi writes, "We stand on the threshold of an age whose convulsions proclaim alike the death-pangs of the old world order and the birth-pangs of the new."

We can see evidence of the decay of the old world order nearly everywhere we look. Religious intolerance, racial strife, and nationalism are increasing. An ever-rising divorce rate and irresponsible attitudes toward marriage are weakening the stability of the family and eroding the foundations of society. Selfishness, suspicion, and fear are growing. Alcoholism, drug abuse, and other self-destructive habits are widespread. Terrorism, lawlessness, and crime are increasing in frequency and severity. Yet, distressing as these signs of moral and social decay are, they are also cause for great hope. They are like the darkest hours of night that come before the dawn of a new day.

Humanity's present state may seem bleak, but we are reminded by Bahá'u'lláh that adversities have prevailed in the beginning of every revelation and later have been turned into great prosperity. Bahá'u'lláh proclaims, "Soon will the present-day order be rolled up, and a new one spread out in its stead." "The whole earth is now in a state of pregnancy. The day is approaching when it will have yielded its noblest fruits, when from it will have sprung forth the loftiest trees, the most enchanting blossoms, the most heavenly blessings." We are assured that "A new life is, in this age, stirring within all the peoples of the earth. . . ."

Universal Participation

Humanity's dire condition calls for heroic efforts to carry Bahá'u'lláh's healing message to every living soul. It is the only message that can truly rescue, uplift, and revive the desperate, suffering masses. The surest way to spread Bahá'u'lláh's message of hope is for every Bahá'í to participate in teaching the Faith, living the Bahá'í life, contributing to the Bahá'í Funds, and continually trying to improve his or her understanding of the significance of Bahá'u'lláh's revelation.

Every Bahá'í has a special role to play in advancing God's Cause. Bahá'u'lláh compares the world of humanity to the human body. Every cell, every organ, and every nerve in the body have a different part to play. No cell—no matter what its role may be—can live apart from the body. When each part does its job, the body is healthy, energetic, and ready to do whatever is needed. The same is true of the body of humanity. "Every believer is of the utmost importance and is a source of power and vitality as yet unknown to us," says the Universal House of Justice. Each of us has a unique set of talents and abilities that can be used to serve the Faith. To restore health and prosperity to the body of humanity, everyone must arise and use those talents and abilities to play his or her part.

Ultimately, the fate of humanity depends on every believer's participation in helping to build the World Order of Bahá'u'lláh. Shoghi Effendi compares the role of the individual to that of a brick in the structure of the Bahá'í Administrative Order, the embryonic World Order of Bahá'u'lláh. Each of us supports and ensures its stability. Wholehearted, generous, and continuous support from every believer makes the structure strong and stable. If even one of us withdraws or relaxes our support, the structure is weakened.

As we arise to play our part, there are ways we can help to encourage others to participate. The Universal House of Justice explains that "The real secret to universal participation" lies in 'Abdu'l-Bahá's often-expressed wish that we should "love each other, constantly encourage each other, work together, be as one soul in one body, and in so doing become a true, organic, healthy body illumined by the spirit." Working together in this spirit, says the Universal House of Justice, gives us "spiritual health and vitality." From such efforts "the most perfect flowers and fruits will be brought forth."

Divine Assistance

If each of us does our part to advance Bahá'u'lláh's Cause, we will be amazed at the power, growth, and blessings that result. Bahá'u'lláh promises His divine assistance to those who arise: "We are with you at all times, and shall strengthen you through the power of truth. We are truly almighty. Whoso hath recognized Me will arise and serve Me with such determination that the powers of earth and heaven shall be unable to defeat his purpose." Furthermore, Bahá'u'lláh promises to watch over us and to "aid whosoever will arise for the triumph of Our Cause with the hosts of the Concourse on high and a company of Our favored angels." To receive His divine assistance, we have only to arise and play our part.

Creating a Personal Plan of Action

There are as many ways to play a part in advancing Bahá'u'lláh's Cause as there are Bahá'ís. In fact, there are so many ways to serve the Faith that we may risk neglecting some of them if we do not have a personal plan of action to guide us. A personal plan of action is like a road map that helps us choose a path of spiritual growth and keeps us moving in the right direction.

Though each of us will set goals according to our own strengths, needs, and interests, everyone's plan of action should include certain basic elements. They include daily prayer and meditation, a personal teaching campaign, personal study and deepening, giving to the Bahá'í Funds, paying Ḥuqúqu'lláh if it is applicable, participating in Bahá'í community life, and supporting the Bahá'í Administrative Order.

To begin creating a personal plan, we may ask ourselves the following questions:

DAILY PRAYER AND MEDITATION

- What will I do to develop the daily habit of prayer and meditation?
- How much time will I set aside for devotions?
- Where is the best place for me to pray and meditate in private?

- Do I need to get up earlier each day to make time for morning devotions?
- What prayers and passages from the Bahá'í writings will I memorize?
- Do I have a Bahá'í prayer book?

PERSONAL TEACHING CAMPAIGN

- What will I do to make my actions mirror my beliefs more tomorrow than they did today?
- How will I make teaching the "dominating passion" of my life?
- Can I set a daily goal to mention Bahá'u'lláh to at least one person I have never met before?
- Have I read 'Abdu'l-Bahá's *Tablets of the Divine Plan*, the plan for teaching the Faith throughout the world?
- Am I able to relate the Bahá'í teachings to contemporary issues?
- How many of my friends and family have not yet heard of Bahá'u'lláh? What will I do about it?
- What special skills and talents can I use to teach the Faith?
- Am I able to go traveling teaching or pioneering here on the homefront or internationally?
- Am I in a position to donate a year of service as a pioneer or traveling teacher?
- If I am not now able to go traveling teaching or pioneering, what can I do to prepare myself for doing so in the future?
- Do I know a language that would enable me to teach non-English-speaking people?
- What can I do that will identify me as a Bahá'í and encourage people to ask me about the Faith?
- Are there meetings I can attend at which I am likely to meet seekers of Bahá'u'lláh's message?
- How often will I hold meetings for seekers in my home, and who will I invite?
- Does my local Bahá'í community have a teaching goal? What will I do to help reach the goal?
- What can I do to help my National Spiritual Assembly accomplish its teaching goals?

- What can I do to help accomplish the teaching goals set by the Universal House of Justice?
- Do I have pamphlets and other teaching materials I can give away to seekers?

PERSONAL STUDY AND DEEPENING

- What Bahá'í writings do 'Abdu'l-Bahá and Shoghi Effendi suggest that we study?
- What Bahá'í writings does my Local Spiritual Assembly suggest I should study first?
- What Bahá'í writings am I interested in studying?
- What aspects of the Faith do I understand the least?
- Have I studied the compilations released by the Universal House of Justice that address topics of particular importance to Bahá'ís?
- Would I like to study alone or with others?
- Which of the permanent, regional, or local Bahá'í schools or institutes can I attend?
- Does my community sponsor deepening classes?
- Would I like to start a study group?
- How often will I study, and when?
- When I study, what will I do to make prayer, meditation, memorization, and action a part of my learning process?

GIVING TO THE BAHÁ'Í FUNDS

- What will I do to remind myself to contribute regularly to all of the Bahá'í Funds?
- What amount will I set as a goal for myself to contribute? Have I included it in my budget?
- Do I know how to make contributions to the local Bahá'í Fund, the National Bahá'í Fund, the Continental Bahá'í Fund, the International Bahá'í Fund, and the Arc Projects Fund? Who will I ask if I am not sure?
- Does my local community have a goal for contributing to the various Funds?
- Do I understand the purpose and significance of building the Arc on Mount Carmel?

- When and how often will I send my contributions to the Funds?
- What sacrifices will I make to give to the Funds?
- Will I participate in the automatic contribution system set up by the National Spiritual Assembly?
- If I cannot go traveling teaching or pioneering, am I able to assist by sending someone in my stead?

OBEYING THE LAW OF ḤUQÚQU'LLÁH

- Do I understand the purpose and significance of the law of Ḥuqúqu'lláh?
- Do I owe Ḥuqúq?

PARTICIPATING IN BAHÁ'Í COMMUNITY LIFE

- Will I resolve to try to attend every Nineteen Day Feast?
- Are there ways I can participate in planning and hosting the Feasts?
- Are there other Bahá'í meetings I can attend?
- Can I open my home for meetings?
- Do I greet and welcome newcomers and visitors to the community?
- Can I help with child care, children's classes, or youth activities?
- Do I have a talent or skill that would benefit the community?
- Do I have time I could use in service to the community?
- Am I in a position to donate a year of community service?
- Can I make it my personal mission to visit those who are sick, lonely, or in need of help?
- What will I do to get more involved in my community?

SUPPORTING THE ADMINISTRATIVE ORDER

- What will I do to deepen my understanding of the Bahá'í Administrative Order, the "nucleus and pattern" of the World Order of Bahá'u'lláh?
- Do I understand the nature, purpose, and spirit of Bahá'í elections?

- Am I ready to arise and serve if I am elected to a Spiritual Assembly or appointed to one of its committees?
- Do I understand the principle of Bahá'í consultation and use it at every opportunity?
- Do I consult with my Local Spiritual Assembly when I am preparing to make an important decision?
- Do I participate in consultation at the Nineteen Day Feast?
- Do I share my concerns and suggestions with the Local Spiritual Assembly? Do I offer useful information when I can?
- What can I do to support and help carry out the Local Spiritual Assembly's plans?

There are no wrong answers to these questions, and we may think of many others we can ask ourselves. As we form a plan of action, we should be sure to take into consideration Bahá'u'lláh's power to reinforce the efforts of those who serve Him, His promise to do so, and the impotence of our efforts without His divine assistance. The goal is to respond thoughtfully and actively to Bahá'u'lláh's counsel to "Arise, O wayfarer in the path of the Love of God, and aid thou His Cause."

The Joyous Journey of Service

As newly enrolled Bahá'ís, we are beginning a lifelong journey of serving Bahá'u'lláh's Cause. God has bestowed on us an inestimable privilege and honor by enabling us to recognize and accept His Manifestation in this matchless Day.

We live in what 'Abdu'l-Bahá describes as "the spring season of God." It is "a day of joy, a time of happiness, a period of spiritual growth." 'Abdu'l-Bahá asks,

Do ye know in what cycle ye are created and in what age ye exist? This is the age of the Blessed Perfection and this is the time of the Greatest Name! This is the century of the Manifestation, the age of the Sun of all horizons and the beautiful springtime of the Eternal One!

. . . If we are not happy and joyous at this season, for what other season shall we wait and for what other time shall we look?

'Abdu'l-Bahá offers the following supplication:

> I beg of God that this divine spiritual civilization may have the fullest impression and effect on you. May you become as growing plants. May the trees of your hearts bring forth new leaves and variegated blossoms. May ideal fruits appear from them in order that the world of humanity, which has grown and developed in material civilization, may be quickened in the bringing forth of spiritual ideals. . . . may minds and spirits . . . come into the knowledge of the verities of God, and the realities of the Kingdom be made manifest in human hearts. Then the world will be the paradise of Abhá, the standard of the Most Great Peace will be borne aloft, and the oneness of the world of humanity in all its beauty, glory and significance will become apparent.

We are blessed with the revelation that has been heralded from time immemorial as the purpose, the promise, and the most cherished desire of every Prophet of God. Bahá'u'lláh refers repeatedly in His writings to the greatness of this Day: "This is the Day in which God's most excellent favors have been poured out upon men, the Day in which His most mighty grace hath been infused into all created things." "This is the Day whereon the Ocean of God's mercy hath been manifested unto men, the Day in which the Day Star of His loving-kindness hath shed its radiance upon them, the Day in which the clouds of His bountiful favor have overshadowed the whole of mankind." We are told in Bahá'u'lláh's writings that this is "the Day in which the fragrances of mercy have been wafted over all created things, a Day so blest that past ages and centuries can never hope to rival it."

Bahá'u'lláh helps us to understand the importance of our service to His Cause. He explains, "This is a Revelation, under which, if a man shed for its sake one drop of blood, myriads of oceans will be his recompense." He has not revealed the exalted station that every true believer can attain, because "the joy which such a revelation must provoke might well cause a few to faint away and die." But Bahá'u'lláh does say that the excellence of His magnificent revelation can help us to imagine the honor with which His faithful followers are invested. He promises, "The very breath of these souls is in itself richer than all the treasures of the earth. Happy is the man that hath attained thereunto. . . ."

Bahá'u'lláh urges us to "Render thanks unto God" for having attained our heart's desire and for having been united with "Him Who is the Promise of all nations." It is now our duty to work calmly, constantly, and confidently to assist, in whatever ways we can, the forces Bahá'u'lláh is gathering and directing to lead humanity toward the heights of power and glory. Let us be "unrestrained as the wind" as we carry the message of "Him Who hath caused the Dawn of Divine Guidance to break." Let us follow Bahá'u'lláh's exhortation to "Unloose your tongues, and proclaim unceasingly His Cause."

Suggested Reading

The materials listed below are available through the Bahá'í Distribution Service. Address inquiries to:

Bahá'í Distribution Service
5397 Wilbanks Drive
Chattanooga, TN 37343

To place an order call: 1-800-999-9019
E-mail address: bds@usbnc.org

Writings of Bahá'u'lláh

Gleanings from the Writings of Bahá'u'lláh. Shoghi Effendi's selection of some of the most characteristic passages from Bahá'u'lláh's writings.
The Hidden Words. A collection of brief, gem-like utterances that set forth the essence of Bahá'u'lláh's ethical teachings.
The Kitáb-i-Aqdas: The Most Holy Book. The charter of Bahá'u'lláh's New World Order and the main repository of the laws and ordinances of His Dispensation.
The Kitáb-i-Íqán: The Book of Certitude. Bahá'u'lláh's explanation of the basic teachings of His Faith and of the continuity of religion.
Tablets of Bahá'u'lláh revealed after the Kitáb-i-Aqdas. A collection of sixteen of Bahá'u'lláh's most significant letters revealed after the Kitáb-i-Aqdas.

Writings of the Báb

Selections from the Writings of the Báb. A selection of the Báb's writings and utterances.

Writings and Utterances of 'Abdu'l-Bahá

Selections from the Writings of 'Abdu'l-Bahá. A compilation of passages from 'Abdu'l-Bahá's letters to the Bahá'ís of the East and West.
Some Answered Questions. A collection of talks 'Abdu'l-Bahá gave in response to questions about a wide range of spiritual and philosophical subjects.
Tablets of the Divine Plan: Revealed by 'Abdu'l-Bahá to the North American Bahá'ís. A collection of fourteen letters to the Bahá'ís of the United States, Canada, and Greenland; 'Abdu'l-Bahá's charter for spreading the Bahá'í Faith throughout the world.

Will and Testament of 'Abdu'l-Bahá. 'Abdu'l-Bahá's charter of a future world civilization. This document is indispensable for a complete understanding of the spirit, mission, and future of the Bahá'í Faith.

Writings of Shoghi Effendi

The Advent of Divine Justice. A letter to the Bahá'ís of the United States and Canada about fulfilling the duties and responsibilities assigned in 'Abdu'l-Bahá's Tablets of the Divine Plan. The letter explains the requirements for success in teaching and living the Bahá'í life and gives practical guidance for coping with the problems of our time.

God Passes By. A history of the first century (1844–1944) of the Bahá'í Dispensation.

Selected Writings of Shoghi Effendi. A compact survey of some of Shoghi Effendi's most powerful writings conveying Bahá'u'lláh's central teachings and His plan for a new world order.

The World Order of Bahá'u'lláh: Selected Letters. A collection of seven major letters presenting a clear vision of the Bahá'í Faith's role in social evolution. The letters challenge Bahá'ís to arise and play their part in the "greatest drama of the world's spiritual history."

Your True Brother: Messages to Junior Youth Written by and on Behalf of Shoghi Effendi, Guardian of the Bahá'í Faith. Eight letters from Shoghi Effendi to young Bahá'ís grappling with questions such as "Who am I?" and "Where am I going?"

Writings of the Universal House of Justice

Individual Rights and Freedoms in the World Order of Bahá'u'lláh: To the Followers of Bahá'u'lláh in the United States of America. A letter from the Universal House of Justice discussing individual rights and freedom of expression within the Bahá'í community.

The Promise of World Peace: To the Peoples of the World. A message to all humanity about the prerequisites of a peaceful global civilization.

Compilations of Bahá'í Writings

Bahá'í Education: A Compilation

Bahá'í Funds: Contributions and Administration

Bahá'í Marriage and Family Life: Selections from the Writings of the Bahá'í Faith

Bahá'í Prayers: A Selection of Prayers Revealed by Bahá'u'lláh, the Báb, and 'Abdu'l-Bahá

Consultation: A Compilation

The Continental Boards of Counselors: Letters, Extracts from Letters, and Cables from The Universal House of Justice; An Address by Edna M. True

The Establishment of the Universal House of Justice

Ḥuqúqu'lláh: Extracts from the Writings of Bahá'u'lláh, 'Abdu'l-Bahá, Shoghi Effendi, and The Universal House of Justice

The Importance of Deepening Our Knowledge and Understanding of the Faith

The Local Spiritual Assembly

The National Spiritual Assembly

The Pattern of Bahá'í Life

Political Non-Involvement and Obedience to Government: A Compilation of Some of the Messages of the Guardian and the Universal House of Justice

Preserving Bahá'í Marriages: A Memorandum and Compilation prepared by the Universal House of Justice

The Sanctity and Nature of Bahá'í Elections: A Compilation of Extracts from the Bahá'í Writings

Spiritual Foundations: Prayer, Meditation, and the Devotional Attitude

Stirring of the Spirit: Celebrating the Institution of the Nineteen Day Feast

Teaching, The greatest gift of God: Extracts from the Writings of Bahá'u'lláh, 'Abdu'l-Bahá, and Shoghi Effendi

Trustworthiness: A Compilation of Extracts from the Bahá'í Writings

Women: Extracts from the Writings of Bahá'u'lláh, 'Abdu'l-Bahá, Shoghi Effendi, and the Universal House of Justice